The Revelation of Jesus Christ, Pertaining to the Kingdom of God

T.F. Igler

NEW HARBOR PRESS

Rapid City, SD

Copyright © 2024 by T.F. Igler.

All rights reserved. No part of this publication may be reproduced, distributed or transmitted in any form or by any means, including photocopying, recording, or other electronic or mechanical methods, without the prior written permission of the publisher, except in the case of brief quotations embodied in critical reviews and certain other noncommercial uses permitted by copyright law. For permission requests, write to the publisher, addressed "Attention: Permissions Coordinator," at the address below.

Igler/New Harbor Press
1601 Mt Rushmore Rd, Ste 3288
Rapid City, SD 57701
http://NewHarborPress.com

Ordering Information:
Quantity sales. Special discounts are available on quantity purchases by corporations, associations, and others. For details, contact the "Special Sales Department" at the address above.

The Revelation of Jesus Christ, Pertaining to the Kingdom of God/T.F. Igler. —1st ed.
ISBN 978-1-63357-457-1

All Scripture quotations are King James Version, italicized, and often with emphasis added. Not all quotes include chapter and verse. Repetitions are intentional and may include the complete text

Contents

Preface 1

Introduction 3

FOUNDATIONAL 5

SIMILITUDES AND PATTERNS 9

REALMS AND PRINCIPALS 15

THE REVELATION 25

REVELATION, CHAPTERS 1–3 27

REVELATION, CHAPTERS 4–5 37

REVELATION, CHAPTER 6 45

REVELATION, CHAPTER 7 49

REVELATION, CHAPTERS 8–9 53

REVELATION, CHAPTER 10 61

REVELATION, CHAPTER 11 63

REVELATION, CHAPTERS 12–13 73

REVELATION, CHAPTERS 14–16 81

REVELATION, CHAPTERS 17–18 89

REVELATION, CHAPTER 19 99

REVELATION, CHAPTER 20 103

REVELATION, CHAPTERS 21–22 107

TABLES 113

Postscript 125

Preface

THE BOOK OF REVELATION is treated with questioning, rejection, and controversy. Much has been published. Likely, the greater volume of commentary has not been published and resides in ceiled houses and other private endeavors. General agreement concerning Revelation's timeline, and the desired knowledge of its many sayings and similitudes is yet to be realized.

Revelation speaks of beginnings and declares God's will, path, and means toward the glorious end of his 'Plan of Restoration.' That understanding, pertaining to mankind's salvation, is our desired pursuit. We, *"according to his promise, look for new heavens and a new earth, wherein dwelleth righteousness"* (King James Version, II Peter 3:13).*

Daniel stated, *"And I heard, but I understood not: then said I, O my Lord, what shall be the end of these things? And he said, Go thy way, Daniel: for the words are closed up and sealed till the time of the end"* (Daniel 12:8–9). That statement tells the reader that God allows revealed truth in time and season. This writer believes that 'the time of the end' draws near and the need to know is in season.

The thundering of God's ending statement to the Gentile world will be heard and felt. The message will be a God-ordained dispensing from heaven; a blended 'authoritative' and timely 'stewardship' of the mystery. At such a time of experiential knowing and revelation, we will stand in awe, fearing wonderfully lest we offend God. As saith the prophet of old: *". . . Write the vision, and make it plain upon tables, that he may run that readeth it. For the vision is yet for an appointed time, but at the end it shall speak, and not lie: though it tarry, wait for it; because it will surely come, it will not tarry"* (Habakkuk 2:2, 3).

Revelation truth will be made known and the actuality of the Revelation events, however surreal, will separate the wheat from the tares, and that by the disposition of the Angels. What remains will be the Church of which Christ is the head. Advancing truth is not a 'deconstruct' of the Christian faith. Quite to the contrary. If church entities are not inclined to hear and heed timely warnings, then, as per the principal, Jesus expressed: *"Go out into the highways and hedges, and compel them to come in, that my house may be filled"* (Luke 14:23). Blessed are they that are found in God's right hand, taken out of that image of worldly civilizations and secured in the unto-eternal-life column. Yea, *"Come out of her, my people, that we be not partakers of her sins, and that ye receive not of her plagues"* (Revelation 18:4).

Introduction

The Apostle writes: *"Knowing this first, that no prophecy of the scripture is of any private interpretation. For the prophecy came not in old time by the will of man: but holy men of God spake as they were moved by the Holy Ghost"* (II Peter 1:20–21).

Prophecy speaks of God's plan and intent. And, their fulfillment eludes carnal understanding. Only God and the heavenly host know the measure of God's intent. *". . . King of kings, and Lord of lords; Who only hath immortality, dwelling in the light which no man can approach unto; whom no man hath seen, nor can see."* (I Timothy 6:15–16). That part which does extend to man is precious and it is divinely 'dispensed.' Such is the calling of the Prophet. To be so possessed by God is man's highest calling and estate.

About one-third of the Bible is prophecy. That makes the Bible the most unique and treasured book on earth. Jude, verse 20, wrote, *"But ye, beloved, building up yourselves on your most holy faith, praying in the Holy Ghost . . ."* Being *"in Christ"* is that same estate as *"praying in the Holy Ghost,"* Revelation is a Book of God's divine Word, gifted to Christ and then conveyed to his people. Ideally, the child of God meditates in Revelation, being *"in the Holy Ghost."* Knowing this, *"the things of God knoweth no man, but the Spirit of God"* (I Corinthians 2:11).

Revelation is a book of prophecy. That being the fact, any commentary added to the study tends to be trivial by comparison. Statements inspired *"in the Holy Ghost"* are exceptional. Revelation gives us visions that are reflections of the 'dispositional' part. That is, more than mere physical phenomena understood by observation. This expositor keeps his commentary to a minimum. Thus, the writing does not qualify as a comprehensive commentary. Not by any means. Not by intention. We humbly desire to exalt the glory of the Revelation and encourage the reader toward contriteness of heart. *"Blessed are they that morn: for they shall be comforted"* (Matthew 5:4). The Revelation of restoration is truly a comfort to the believer.

Progressing through Revelation, we will see the revealing of two bodies; an 'outside the body of Christ,' or false church, and an 'in the body of Christ,' or true church. Respectively, *"he that had the mark, or the name of the beast, or the number of his name"* versus those *"having his Father's name written in their foreheads"* (Revelation 13:17, 14:1). That equates to the *"thy* (serpent) *seed and her* (woman) *seed"* (Genesis 3:15).

False religion guides the masses and that is a 'hell' condition. To wit: *"the great whore that sitteth upon many waters."* And, *"The waters which thou saweth, where the whore sitteth, are peoples, and multitudes, and nations, and tongues"* (Revelation 17:1, 15). Daniel 2:31–35 depicts the ungodly civilizations as a *"great image."* The godly are admonished: *"Here is wisdom. Let him that hath understanding count the number of the beast: for it is the number of a man; and his number is Six hundred threescore and six."* (Revelation 13:18).

CHAPTER I

FOUNDATIONAL

"THE REVELATION OF JESUS CHRIST" (Revelation 1:1). The Lord does allow the embrace of his *"Word."* However, the required state is faith-believing. There is no place for pride or doubt. This is our humble confession. And, that is the Higher Ground toward 'knowing.' Please be encouraged in your faith. Resist giving up the search or relegating the matter to no-need-to-know. Turn aside from a worldly mindset and apply yourself to the prayerful study at hand. On the point of dedication and discipline, Jesus said, *"The children of this world* (like the unjust steward) *are in their generation wiser than the children of light"* (Luke 16:8). Paul stated, *"And every man that striveth for the mastery is temperate in all things. Now they* (the children of this world) *do it to obtain a corruptible crown; but we an incorruptible"* (I Corinthians 9:25).

There must not be a lifting-up of any writing or proponent of any school of thought. The mandate is to enter the room of *"those which do hunger and thirst after righteousness,"* and *"him that is poor and of a contrite spirit, and trembleth at my word"* (Matthew 5:6, Isaiah 66:2). It is our calling to be that *"place"* where Jesus rests his head. His house will be built, howbeit, in troublous times. The more clarion sound, or admonition, is that we search with our Holy Ghost, *"Christ in you,"* leading the way. We humbly confess that we are given passage only as being *"made the righteousness of God in him"* (Colossians 1:27, II Corinthians 5:21).

THE UNVEILING OF REVELATION MYSTERIES WILL BE EMBRACED FIRST BY THE CHURCH. Necessary, greater understanding will be introduced into the Church during the three and one-half years preceding the 'last hour.' That will be the esoteric part, when the Lord works primarily, not exclusively, with his church ministry. That is a preparatory operation leading into the Latter Rain church operation. Call it the in-house phase, when the Church begins functioning more perfectly. Again, that three and one-half years will be the up-front season of the Latter Rain Gentile church operation. Thereafter, begins the season of three and one-half years dispensing of the fullness of the gifts of the ministry; the time of the Latter Rain concluding message to the Gentile age. The total being seven years. (The Early Rain comparable is the three and one-half years from Christ's baptism till his crucifixion and the day of Pentecost. Then, forward from Pentecost, the three and one-half years of Early Rain ministry to the Jews concluded with the martyrdom of Stephen. That total also being seven years.)

Revelation reveals the manner of exodus from the wrath of God and soon coming annihilation of first heaven and first earth; furthermore, transitioning into the new heaven and new earth. Jesus paid the price of redemption, his life's blood, allowing for mankind's at-one-ment with his creator. Jesus is our atonement. And, Revelation's message of judgment and redemption was dispensed by way of John obediently recording the vision. The at-one-ment is vital in gaining the truth of the book of Revelation and our exodus from the wrath of God. The better part is that the 'blessed' are sacrificial, holiness unto the Lord and favored participants in his plan of the ages. The apostle Paul stated, *". . . Eye hath not seen, nor ear heard, neither have entered into the heart of man, the things which God hath prepared for them that love him. But God hath revealed them unto us by his Spirit: for the Spirit searcheth all things, yea, the deep things of God. For what man knoweth the things of a man, save the spirit of man which is in him? Even so the things of God knoweth no man, but the Spirit of God"* (I Corinthians 2:9–11). Jesus is our atonement, with the right of citizenship into the estate of *"in Christ Jesus,"* even into *"a new heaven and a new earth."*

Fallen mankind has its worldview. That vision is sundry, varied, and *". . . seemeth right unto a man, but the end thereof are the ways of death"* (Proverbs 14:12). Revelation's understanding gives forth God's prescription for life everlasting and the prophesied demise of man's worldview. All that lives into eternity will walk according to the way of God; a faithful subscriber to Christ's example. *"But now being made free from sin, and become servants to God, ye have your fruit unto holiness, and the end everlasting life"* (Romans 6:22). Speaking of the saints: *"In whom we have redemption through his blood, the forgiveness of sins, according to the riches of his grace; Wherein he hath abounded toward us in all wisdom and prudence; Having made known unto us the mystery of his will, according to his good pleasure which he hath purposed in himself: That in the dispensation of the fullness of times he might gather together in one all things in Christ, both which are in heaven, and which are on earth; even in him"* (Ephesians 1:7–10).

DANIEL 9:24 STATES, *"Seventy weeks are determined upon thy people and upon thy holy city, (1) to finish the transgression, and (2) to make an end of sins, and (3) to make reconciliation for iniquity, and (4) to bring in everlasting righteousness, and (5) to seal up the vision and prophecy, and (6) to anoint the most Holy."* These six mentions were *"determined,"* on the cross, when Jesus said, *"It is finished"* (John 19:30). A seventh item was not mentioned. To wit: *"the times of restitution of all things, which God hath spoken by the mouth of all his holy prophets since the world began"* (Acts 3:21). That part was not in the purview of Daniel's prophesying. That part was sealed and awaits our time. To wit: The revealing and dispensing of the understanding of the book of Revelation: *"The Revelation of Jesus Christ"* (Revelation 1:1).

The above fifth mention was *"seal up the vision and prophecy."* Again, that was determined on the cross and the unveiling was held in reserve for the future time and season. The book of Revelation addresses the future, latter phase of God's plan for the "restitution of all things." Revelation 5:5 reads *"the Lion of the tribe of Judah, the Root of David, hath prevailed to open the book, and to loose the seven seals thereof."* The opening of the book and loosing of the seals progress as Christ's life and sacrifice allowed. Thus, the revealing of end-time judgments and the message of restitution. Beginning with the fourth chapter of Revelation, John writes prophetically of a future privilege; future to John's time but near future for this generation.

God-ordained stewardship, or dispensing of truth, will equate to sacrifice. That is the nature of the mandate. Thus, we speak of the privilege of giving our lives, figuratively and literally, to declare the good news of the gospel. It is God who sits on the throne of heaven and dispenses all things that are righteous and good. The Revelation was God's gift, or dispensing, to Christ. And, Christ was God's gift to mankind. The Revelation is Christ's gift to the Church.

The book of Revelation portrays the end product of Christ's role as Judge of all things. Earlier, the same writer John stated the words of Jesus: *"For the Father judgeth no man, but hath committed all judgment unto the Son: That all men should honour the Son, even as they honour the Father"* (John 5:22–23). Referencing judgment, Jude, verse 9, states, *"Yet Michael the archangel, when contending with the devil he disputed about the body of Moses, durst not bring against him a railing accusation, but said, The Lord rebuke thee."* Jesus' life and sacrificial death were future to Michael's contest with the devil. Jesus' death on the cross did bruise the serpent's head. He is God's only Atonement for creature and creation. Jesus established God's righteousness so that without his atonement there is no forgiveness. There is no 'universal' salvation and there is no liberal 'umbrella' of peace outside of Jesus Christ. *"The vile person shall be no more called liberal, nor the churl said to be bountiful"* (Isaiah 32:5). The reader is encouraged to read Isaiah chapter 32.

REGARDING THE TEXT: Revelation reads as a continuous revelatory event and a singular unbroken recording of that experience. While we reasonably consider the twenty-two-chapter volume of visions and discourse to be beyond anyone's capacity of a one-time happening and reporting, there is no doubt God could have miraculously given John the capacity to see, hear, and write the Revelation from a one-time giving of the vision. Revelation is to be treated as one writing and should be embraced as one work. Confessing that, we do see the Vision being dispensed over a period of time. We note that chapter 4 begins with *"After this . . ."* Thus, a departure from addressing churches contemporary with John, thence forward, addressing future events. The question arises: Can that juncture also indicate a time break of John receiving and recording the vision, thus gaining the total in parts, as per a compilation? Whether the breaks are stated, or textually indicated, there is the likelihood that Revelation, in total, is a compilation. John received visions of the same event, repeated to him from different realms and at different times. Accordingly, this writing will incorporate jumping-ahead snippets as well as repetitions of Revelation Scripture. Obviously, same events would occupy the same time slot on a timeline.

JESUS IS THE CHRIST OF GOD. Jesus Christ is the ever-present foundation of the book of Revelation. That understanding is to the glory of God. Christ existed before he was born of his earthly sojourn. *"In the beginning was the Word, and the Word was with God, and the Word was God"* (John 1:1). God's *"Word"* embodied Jesus Christ. In that sense, God's 'intent' was the womb and symbolically the mother of Christ. Jesus was the first creation of God. As such, being created, God had 'intent' before the happening of his creation. From the beginning, Jesus was referred to as the *'wisdom'* of the Father. See Proverbs 8. It depicts Christ and God's good pleasure to reveal him as 'man,' thus manifesting himself to mankind; unto their salvation.

REVELATION'S *"SEALS"* ARE GOD'S ORDERS, and their dispensing unto mankind resides with Christ. Jesus is the Son of God. Jesus is the *"Alpha and Omega"* of prophecy. So being, past and ongoing, Jesus continues ever-present with the Father. That is Christ's estate; ever-present with the Father. Christ is the Son of God and he is 'resident' as family. Restating the premises: God is omnipresent and his *"Word,"* plan, and intent are likewise omnipresent. The precious gift of knowing God's *"Word"* lifts Jesus higher. The more we understand the glory of the mystery, the more we love and revere our Lord and Savior. He is God manifest to mankind. Jesus is Lord and he is our savior and soon-coming King. Revelation is God's prophesied plan. *Prophecy,* being a 'statement' of God's intent, and *Christ,* being the 'fulfillment' of God's intent, together, is a perfect unity. To wit: *"The testimony of Jesus is the spirit of prophecy"* (Revelation 19:10).

CHAPTER II

SIMILITUDES AND PATTERNS

APPLICABLE COMPARABLES facilitate the interpreting of Revelation. These are revelatory, necessary, and best embraced from the onset of the study. Consider them as prerequisites toward understanding the timeline, events, and even the mindset of the Lord as set forth in the book of Revelation. These are given early on and not in a glossary or addendum. Related thoughts are included with their mention. *'Related thoughts'* are jumping-ahead snippets touching facts that are expounded upon later in the text; often prefaced with the notation *'to wit.'*

Similitudes and patterns are the beginning body of our study of Revelation.

SIMILITUDE: INCLUSIVE IN THE SEVENTH IS SEVEN. The capture of Jericho related in the book of Joshua, chapter 6, gives us the principle of the seventh being seven. *"Now Jericho was straitly shut up because of the children of Israel: none went out, and none came in. And the LORD said unto Joshua, See, I have given into thine hand Jericho, and the king thereof, and the mighty men of valor. And ye shall compass the city, all ye men of war, and go round about the city once. Thus shalt thou do six days. And seven priests shall bear before the ark seven trumpets of rams' horns: and the seventh day ye shall compass the city seven times, and the priests shall blow the trumpets. And it shall come to pass, that when they make a long blast with the ram's horn, and when ye hear the sound of the trumpet, all the people shall shout with a great shout; and the wall of the city shall fall down flat, and the people shall ascend up every man straight before him"* (Joshua 6:1–5).

Joshua and company compassed the city six times with a day's separation. That occupied six days. The seventh day they marched around the city seven times, the trumpets sounded and with a shout, the walls fell. A bold, fearless, and unerring resolve was demonstrated in the event of Jericho. That is noteworthy. It shows the Spirit and flavor of Revelation's prophesied seventh Angel, seventh seal, dispensing seven thunders and seven vials.

To wit: Revelation, chapters 5 and 6, show the opening of the six seals occurring in the time frame of six, almost seven years. Call it *six plus*. The *'plus'* being the time of the final Gentile world war, the Rapture, and the dispersing of the remanent church. The seventh seal, trumpeted, will occupy seven and one-half years, and will be the season of the seven thunders declaring the seven vials of his wrath. This is the third woe of the declaration: *"Woe, woe, woe, to the inhabiters of the earth by reason of the other voices of the trumpet of the three angels, which are yet to sound"* (Revelation 8:13). Again; Revelation reveals that the *"seventh,"* being seven, is the *"third woe,"* the time and season of the wrath of God; seven thunders and seven vials.

SIMILITUDE: ABRAHAM, ISAAC, ELIEZER, HEBRON, AND SARAH'S TENT. Hebron was the dwelling place of Abraham and Sarah at the time Isaac took Rebekah into his mother's tent, signifying a marriage event. *"And Isaac brought her into his mother Sarah's tent, and took Rebekah, and she became his wife* (Genesis 24:67). This was subsequent to Abraham sending his servant, believed to be Eliezer, to *". . . go unto my country, and to my kindred, and take a wife unto my son Isaac"* (Genesis 23:4).

Abraham is likened to God and Isaac is likened to his son Jesus Christ. Eliezer is likened to the Holy Spirit. The Holy Spirit facilitated the union. The applicable New Testament Scripture is: *"As many as are led by the Spirit of God, they are the sons of God"* (Romans 8:14). Hebron is likened unto heaven where the marriage takes place. The events at Sarah's tent, in Hebron, is likened to Christ's union with his bride in heaven.

To wit: *"The marriage of the Lamb is come"* (Revelation 19:7). The marriage supper of the Lamb is a grand celebratory event. It occupies seven and one-half years. It is a definitive dispensing of God's glorious plan and intent. It is a dispensation, however brief, and it occupies a season and it is a perfect reflection of his *"Word,"* dispensed in completeness to the Elect of God. The marriage supper event elevates her from *"man child"* to her later-revealed status of *"the bride, the Lamb's wife"* (Revelation 12:5, 21:9).

Touching a great truth, Sarah's tent is likened unto Heavenly Jerusalem, *"the mother of us all"* (Galatians 4:26). The whole matter conforms to God's divine plan. And, in context, *"Thou art worthy, O LORD, to receive glory and honor and power: for thou hast created all things, and for thy pleasure they are and were created"* (Revelation 4:11).

SIMILITUDE: DAVID'S REIGN AND CHRIST'S REIGN. Concerning the prophesied Christ, Isaiah 9:7 states, *"Of the increase if his government and peace there shall be no end, upon the throne of David, and upon his kingdom, to order it, and to establish it with judgment and with justice from henceforth even for ever. The zeal of the LORD of host will perform this."* The New Testament affirms the same prophecy by the mouth of the angel Gabriel, *"And the angel said unto her, Fear not, Mary: for thou hast found favour with God. And, behold, thou shalt conceive in thy womb, and bring forth a son, and shalt call his name JESUS. He shall be great, and shall be called the Son of the Highest: and the LORD GOD shall give unto him the throne of his father David: And he shall reign over the house of Jacob for ever; and of his kingdom there shall be no end"* (Luke 1:30–33).

David is a type of Christ. This principal understanding is generally recognized, and it is primary, even as a similitude applied in the timeline reckoning in the book of Revelation.

SIMILITUDE: THE DETAIL REGARDING DAVID'S REIGN. David reigned forty years. The first seven and one-half years of his reign was in Hebron. It is recognized, and duly noted, that those seven and one-half years were inclusive of his forty-year reign. *"David was thirty years old when he began to reign, and he reigned forty years. In Hebron he reigned over Judah seven years and six months: and in Jerusalem he reigned thirty and three years over all Israel and Judah"* (II Samuel 5:4, 5).

To wit: Revelation treats Christ's reign as a millennial rule of one thousand years, or the seventh day. The initiation of this beginning is noted by the catching away, or rapture, being the first resurrection. *"And they heard a great voice from heaven saying unto them, come up hither. And they ascended up to heaven in a cloud; and their enemies beheld them"* (Revelation 11:12).

Revelation 11:14–15 announces Christ's reign thus: *"The second woe is past; and, behold, the third woe cometh quickly. And the seventh angel sounded; and there were great voices in heaven, saying, the kingdoms of this world are become the kingdoms of our Lord, and of his Christ; and he shall reign for ever and ever."*

King David's forty-year reign began with the seven-and-one-half year reign in Hebron. Hebron equates to heaven; that being a true similitude, we can affirm Christ's reign begins with *"ascended up to heaven,"* the Rapture. Thus begins the millennial reign of Christ and the seven- and-one-half year marriage supper of the Lamb.

The rapture, beginning the seven-and-one-half year in heaven with those caught-away saints, initiates the time of the third woe mentioned earlier in Revelation 11:14; concurrently, the time of the marriage supper of the Lamb in heaven. It is on the front end of Christ's one-thousand-year day of the Lord. To wit: *". . . They lived and reigned with Christ a thousand years"* (Revelation 20:4). It is the time of the seventh seal and the seventh angel; the thundering from heaven of seven vials of plagues poured into the earth. The Armageddon 'war event' marks the ending of the third woe, being the seventh vial; the seventh of seven. Repeating: Thunders denote that the matter is issued from heaven into the earth. The seven thunders declare that the seven vials, the wrath of God, are ordered of God. 'Armageddon' may be understood to be a protracted seven-and-one-half year dispensing of seven thunders and seven vials, concurrent with the gathering for the war 'event.' Again, the Armageddon 'war event' marks the end, when Christ takes occupancy of Jerusalem, concluding the time of the marriage supper of the Lamb. The Armageddon 'war event' is the conclusion, happening seven and one-half years into the millennium, seventh day. (Obviously, this interpretation lends itself to a pre-tribulation rapture.)

PATTERN: THE EARLY RAIN AND LATTER RAIN COMPARABLE. The Early Rain church narrative, in the overview, started with the birth of Christ. The timeline starts with John the Baptist baptizing Jesus in Jordan. John was of the Law and served as the 'Transition Prophet.' His ministry facilitated the transition from 'Law' to 'Grace.' Jesus was the 'fulfilling of the Law' from his birth, and he was of Divine Origin, so that he was not born under any semblance of the curse of sin. We know that the Law *". . . was added because of transgressions"* (Galatians 3:19). The point being: The time of innocence, freedom from sin and the Law, started with Jesus' birth. In an esoteric sense, Grace was actuated at his baptism in Jordan. John the Baptist said, *"He must increase, but I must decrease. He that cometh from above is above all: he that is of the earth is earthly, and speaketh of the earth: he that cometh from heaven is above all"* (John 3:30–31). Jesus' shed blood on Calvary, then Pentecost, caused that *"the grace of God that bringeth salvation hath appeared to all men"* (Titus 2:11). Thus began the three and one-half years, exoteric, Early Rain.

To wit: The Latter Rain dispensation is on the horizon. As stated earlier, the beginning three and one-half years is the esoteric, in-house, operation when Christ reveals himself to a select few. This writer sees that 'select' being seven principal persons. apostles of Christ. Going forward, many believers are chosen, oriented, and acclimated toward a more perfect Church operation. Then, the initiation of the exoteric church operation. Some think that juncture will be marked by a Latter Rain 'Pentecost' event. Thus, the comparable to the Early Rain;

three and one-half years in-house operation, and then, Pentecost initiated the three and one-half years message, witness, to the Jewish world.

PATTERN: THE EARLY CHURCH DISPENSATION was spiritually profited by the ongoing giving of detailed truth. It was dispensed according to the principle of 'stewardship.' The apostle John ends his Gospel with the statement, *"And there are also many other things which Jesus did, the which, if they should be written every one, I suppose that even the world itself could not contain the books that should be written. Amen"* (John 21:25). John sees an open door for further expression pertaining to the things not recorded. And, the second witness did further expound on the Gospel. As saith Hebrews 2:3; *"How shall we escape, if we neglect so great salvation; which at the first began to be spoken by the Lord* (first witness)*, and was confirmed unto us by them that heard him* (second witness).*"*

To wit: Pertaining to the study of Revelation, this is a baseline principle that says the Gospel is meant to be an increasing revelation in the hearts of believers. Understanding this: New growth will not compromise the fact that his Church is *". . . built upon the foundation of the apostles and prophets, Jesus Christ himself being the chief Cornerstone"* (Ephesians 2:20).

PATTERN: EARLY AND LATTER WITNESS; LIKE FEARS AND LIKE PASSIONS. *"The fear of the Lord"* (Isaiah 11:2) is one of the seven spirits of God. Fearing, lest we fail to *"built upon the foundation of the apostles and prophets, Jesus Christ being the chief corner stone"* (Ephesians 2:20). An end-time ministry innately fears God, with the like-fear peculiar to the watchman on the wall: *"So thou, O son of man, I have set thee a watchman unto the house of Israel; therefore thou shalt hear the word at my mouth, and warn them from me . . . if thou doest not speak to warn the wicked from his way, that wicked man shall die in his iniquity; but his blood will I require at thine hand"* (Ezekiel 33:7–8).

PATTERN: THE INCIDENT OF THE GARDEN OF EDEN; THE FALL AND RAMIFICATIONS. First things first: Adam and Eve were deceived in their *'pride of life,'* the mother of all sin. The result was the breach of their Spirit-spirit communion with God. That action spawned *'enmity,'* the mother of all curses. Fundamentally, enmity is 'death' and causal for war, pestilence, and famine. And, God will use war, pestilence, and famine to purge mankind of sin. Adam and Eve fell further to yielding to their unhinged psyche to the lust of the flesh. Anything not Spirit-spirit connected will gravitate to being a flesh-driven psyche, soul. They were disobedient. Their will ceased being subject to God's will. The penalty was a loss of God-given dominion, including both the plant and animal kingdoms; micro and macro. The result: pestilence and famine. Revelation reveals this phenomenon.

To wit: The book of Revelation is the story of the undoing of Adam's world. That equates to *"the first heaven and the first earth were passed away"* (Revelation 21:1). This comparable is pertinent because the book of Revelation is God's judgment for sin and his prescription for redemption and restoration. These things are in the hand of the rider of the white horse. That is Christ, who is the head of the Church, whose officiation declares these things to mankind. That is the Lord's doing. That 'phenomenon,' and declaration is given for the Church's dispensing unto the earth. It is an integral part of the Church's three-and-one-half year Latter Rain message. That is, the dispensation of the four horses, the first four seals opened in heaven, and then trumpeted into the earth. Christ rides the white horse and he has right of judgment. The red horse being war. The black horse being famine, and the pale horse being pestilence and death.

PATTERN: THE TABERNACLE IN THE WILDERNESS. During the time of Moses and the Law, the tabernacle was an *"in the world . . . not of the world"* estate. It was God's prescription for the salvation of fallen mankind. And, like Eden, it was that place of communion between Creator and creature. The tabernacle in the wilderness shows us three compartments. The Holiest, the Holy Place, and the Courts. Likewise, the book of Revelation shows us three realms. First, the highest realm, or third heaven, where God and the heavenlies emanate forth. The second realm is what can be termed *God's will be done in earth.* Presently, it is the second heaven, Church realm. A heavenly place. Third and lastly, the first heaven realm. Revelation terms this last realm as 'first heaven and the first earth.' It is the earth and its civilizations. Like the body, soma, it is not definitively good or evil. The tabernacle in the wilderness shows us three compartments. Respectively, the Holiest, the Holy Place, and the Courts.

Regarding this pattern: It is helpful if the reader has an understanding of Spirit, Soul, and Body. The principal is stated early on in Scripture. *"And the Lord God formed man of the dust of the ground, and breathed into his nostrils the breath of life; and man became a living soul"* (Genesis 2:7). The *"breath of life"* equates to spirit. *"Living soul"* is clearly stated; soul. And, *"dust of the earth"* equates to the body. Being formed of the dust of the ground and given the breath of life were both the gift of God. That is why Paul said in I Corinthians 6:20, *". . . Glorify God in your body, and in your spirit, which are God's."* As pertaining to this thought; water baptism and Spirit baptism are freely given as were the dust of the ground and the breath of life. When Moses penned the statement *"became a living soul,"* he reveals a thinking person who acts according to the individual's intent. That 'ownership' is ordained of God. He has what we term 'free moral agency.' The soul is where the fire burns. So being, the baptism of fire pertains to the soul or individuality; mind, will, emotions. When the Spirit is in the lead and the individual's spirit is Spirit-spirit connected, that Holy Ghost-led person is perfected as per God's intent. The Holy Ghost facilitates the overcoming process. The fire burns; purging and perfecting.

To wit: The mind is renewed, the will is submitted, and the emotions move from fleshly to fruits of the spirit. Interestingly, Acts 2:3 states, *". . . Cloven tongues like as of fire, and it sat upon each of them."* Clearly, they were 'initiates' into the baptism of fire. There is plausible argument that the baptism of the Holy Ghost and the baptism of Fire are 'effectually' one baptism. That is only true in the life of a person who is obedient to the mandate of Spirit-led fire baptism purging of sin.

Restating the premise: Baptisms are brought into the discussion as a connected fact. Water baptism pertains to the body and it is a physical act (Courts). Spirit baptism is a spirit phenomenon (Holiest). Fire baptism is the purging, new-man phenomenon of renewing the mind, submission of the will, and emotional change from works of the flesh to fruits of the Spirit (Holy Place).

CHAPTER III

REALMS AND PRINCIPALS

THE REVELATION VISIONS emanated from different realms and addressed different principals.

From where does the message emanate forth, and to whom? The highest is 'Spirit realm.' From there the will of God is 'declared.' The second realm includes the collective, Ecclesia, "in the world but not of the world" church operation. From there the message of 'reconciliation,' goes forth. There is a third realm of the world. It is the fallen estate without God's covering or blessing. It has no voice. The worldly realm is void of speech, judgment, or mediation. There is no Spirit connection to the earthly, fleshly, carnal operation. That world is going to pass away. Scripture declares, *"The first heaven and the first earth were passed away . . ."* Note: It is true that the 'earth' can be used as a synonym for 'world.' This present 'world of sin' is going to pass away, but the earth, in the literal, physical sense, is not going to pass away.

THE TABERNACLE OF MOSES DEMONSTRATES THREE REALMS: From the previous chapter, "Pattern: Tabernacle in the Wilderness," the Courts, the Holy Place, and the Holiest were brought to light relating to body, soul, and spirit, respectively. The similitudes being the estates or realms of first heaven, second heaven, and third heaven, respectively. Entering the eastern side gate; first, the Courts and the covering's color was red. Then, through a curtain into the Holy Place and the covering's color was purple. Finally, through the veil into the Holiest of Holies and the covering's color was blue.

THE REALM OF THE WORLD OR THE EARTHLY HABITATION: The 'Courts' reflect the physical, material, bodily part. *"Body,"* translated from *"soma,"* implied no determination as to good or evil. 'Flesh,' translated from the Greek word *'sarx,'* implies carnality, even evil. The 'Court' of the tabernacle in the wilderness shows the offering of blood, sacrifice, and dying. The Court reflects red. Accordingly, the "woes" pertain to this fallen estate. The reader may see the earthly part as so much blood, burning flesh, and tears. Looking at the judgment brought to bear in the process of getting things righted, we can agree with that assessment, as per the present 'fallen' estate. That is why we color it red. God will use those early curses of Genesis 3 to purge the earth. Better said, purging of Adam's first heaven and first earth. Again, the earth, the globe, will not be destroyed, but the face of the earth will be wonderfully changed following the purging by God's wrath. In this we see the unmitigated wrath of God, being the third woe, constituting seven vials and seven thunders; blue on red, with no mediation.

The overriding curse is *enmity,* the separation of mankind from the Creator. That separation of fallen man includes the imposition of another headship. Jesus termed it *"the prince of this world."* Paul termed it, *"the god of this world"* (John 16:11, II Corinthians 4:4). All things carnal are adversarial to the Creator. Therein lies the curse; warfare, destruction, famine, pestilence and death. Specifically, Adam's loss of dominion cost him the productivity of food. That equates to famine. He lost dominion over animal life, macro and micro. That equates to pestilence, disease, the beasts of the earth, and all manner of plagues. Death rules. *"The last enemy that shall be destroyed is death."* That is the present affirmation that death rules in Adam's world. The downside, in the finality, will reveal the upside. The upside is that the burning, the destruction, the wrath of God, is the blessing, netting the restitution of all things. Remember John 3:16; that part that says, whosoever believeth in him should not perish? The corollary of that statement declares whosoever that believeth not shall perish. When sin and death and unbelief are perished, all things are then relegated to the second death. Thus, the first heaven and the first earth are over; it is done. Jesus rides the white horse. His edicts and the resulting judgments are the purging of all things. Even now, spiritual understanding shows us the finality of God's goodness and righteousness. A world wherein dwelleth righteousness.

THE "HOLY PLACE" REALM: The applicable, humanly observed similitude is the tabernacle in the wilderness. The Holy Place operation facilitates the trumpets, the voice of God, speaking from a heavenly estate unto the earth. This present world affords no such realm, which realm exists only in the Church estate, where it is 'in the world but not of the world.' Job would have termed this operation as the *"daysman"* or umpire. From here the heavenly vision is dispensed into the earth. That mission can rightly be termed the dispensation of the Latter Rain church.

To wit: The heavenly vision is trumpeted, manifest, or dispensed, from heaven into the earth; *"And the seven angels which had the seven trumpets prepared themselves to sound"* (Revelation 8:6). Seven trumpets are sounded. The first four pertain to the three-and-one-half year Church, 'Holy Place,' operation: *"And I saw seven angels which stood before God; and to them were given seven trumpets"* (Revelation 8:2). The trumpets are the declarations of things in heaven; setting forth judgments in the earth. The seals are things determined in heaven and the trumpets are the manifest setting-forward of those things. The first four trumpets are judgments and sacrifice, and that with salt having savor. They are ordered of God and declared and accomplished by the officiation of the church. Again, those four soundings included judgment unto salvation; judgments having the flavor of salvation. Sacrifices salted with salt having savor is good. Repeating: That happens in the three-and-one-half-year message of the Latter Rain church. It is the time when the four angels, holding the four winds and doing one-third 'hurt,' being a unity with the 'officiation' of the Church.

The remaining three trumpets sound three *"woes."* There are "woes" attached to the fifth, sixth, and the seventh seals/trumpets. A *'woe'* is judgment lacking the flavor of salvation and void of hope. They are declarations to the 'courts,' the body of lost humanity. The first four trumpets caused one-third 'hurt.' The fifth trumpet or first woe, is a 'hurt not.' It is a pause of judgment on the earth, terra, when the 'sealing' takes place. The sixth trumpet or second woe, the angels are 'loosed' to again 'hurt.' The hurts speak of war, pestilence, and famine on earth, and then, the blood of mankind. The better part of the destruction is that it accomplishes a purging of things pertaining to fallen man and the present world of iniquity. For the Elect, it includes martyrdom. To the otherwise multitude of overcomers, called the woman, it is a time of the Lord's keeping and nourishing her in her place. God's judgments are trumpeted from the highest through the voice of messengers, man, and heavenly angels, into the earth and unto mankind.

Positionally, in Christ, we have that connection and mandate. We are positioned, by faith, to inherit that blessed estate. Our names are written in heaven. That promise and that oath are immutable. The apostle Peter made a connected statement in I Peter 2:5, *"Ye also, as lively stones, are built up a spiritual house, an holy priesthood, to offer up spiritual sacrifices, acceptable to God by Jesus Christ."* The difference is that Peter is referring to things pertaining to the Church; an 'ecclesia,' in the world, but not of the world. These Scriptures are brought forward here because they help make this point: Presently the Church, on earth, reflects God's plan in the heavens. Again, our mandate is to reflect heaven's 'orders.'

THE THRONE OF GOD. THE "HOLIEST" REALM AND PRINCIPALS: God is Spirit. The highest realm is 'Spirit.' From there goes forth his Divine Will and Utterance. God's statements, or directives, are veiled in darkness, as carnally perceived. God is Spirit, and thus, his revelation to us reflects the 'dispositional' aspect of what is otherwise literal. An embrace of Revelation requires that we be spiritually minded, not carnal. And, that is with the Holy Ghost assisting. In Revelation 4:1, John was told *"come up hither."* He rightfully acknowledged: *"And immediately I was in the spirit."* The apostle Paul relates a like-experience. His comment: *"I knew a man in Christ above fourteen years ago, (whether in the body, I cannot tell; or whether out of the body, I cannot tell: God knoweth;) such an one caught up to the third heaven. How that he was caught up into paradise, and heard unspeakable words, which it is not lawful for a man to utter"* (II Corinthians 12:2, 4). It is possible that Paul's statement in Hebrews 9:5 concerning the cherubim, *"of which we cannot now speak particularly,"* may have been referring to a comparable spiritual understanding with an attached 'ineffability factor.' Revelation relates one such restraint; a voice from heaven told John, *"Seal up those things which the seven thunders uttered, and write them not"* (Revelation 10:4).

ONE THAT SAT ON THE THRONE: *"And he that sat was to look upon like a jasper and a sardine stone: and there was a rainbow round about the throne, in sight like unto an emerald"* (Revelation 4:3). Ephesians 4:6 states it thus: *"One God and Father of all, who is above all, and through all, and in you all."*

TWENTY-FOUR ELDERS: *"And round about the throne were four and twenty seats: and upon the seats I saw four and twenty elders sitting, clothed in white raiment; and they had on their heads crowns of gold"* (Revelation 4:4). These twenty-four elders are portrayed as actual entities in the last verses of the chapter. They worshipped God and cast their crowns before the throne. Beyond the likelihood of them being individuals, they represented the twenty-four orders of the Levitical priesthood; the dispensation of 'Law.' The elders reflected the Law which dealt with forgiveness of 'committed sin.' Jesus was the fulfillment of the Law; so being, he could forgive committed sin. Jesus made that fact obvious on one occasion. *"But that ye may know that the Son of man hath power on earth to forgive sins, (he saith to the sick of palsy,) I say unto thee, Arise, and take up thy bed, and go thy way unto thine house"* (Mark 2:10–11). Jesus embodied the Law. Jesus fulfilled the Law. That is why it was said that *"he shall cause the sacrifice* (daily sacrifice) *and oblation to cease."* When Christ died on the cross, the efficacy of animal blood sacrifice became of no effect. Again, the twenty-four elders reflect the Law.

FOUR BEASTS (FOUR LIVING CREATURES): The mention of the four beasts is prefaced by a reference to *"lightnings and thunderings and voices: and there were seven lamps of fire burning before the throne, which are the seven Spirits of God"* (Revelation 4:5). Later in the text, it is made plainer that this is the setting of the atonement, the prophesied Christ, the Lamb, and that is Jesus. *"And before the throne there was a sea of glass like unto crystal: and in the midst of the throne, and round about the throne, were four beasts full of eyes before and behind"* (Revelation 4:6). The text indicates the four beasts were more central to the throne of God than the twenty-four elders. Verse 7 gives symbolisms to the four beasts. *"The first beast was like a lion, and the second beast like a calf, and the third beast had a face as a man, and the fourth beast was like a flying eagle."* Furthermore, the beasts had six wings and they were full of eyes. They had covering, and they had mobility, and they had promises. Matthew shows Christ fulfilling prophecy; the 'lion' of the tribe of Judah. He was sacrificial, as a 'calf,' in Mark. The writings in Luke portray him as 'man.' In John, his divinity is evident. On that point, the 'flying eagle' is exceptional.

A BOOK WRITTEN WITHIN AND ON THE BACKSIDE, SEALED WITH SEVEN SEALS: This equates to his *"Word"* (John 1:1). In the grand view, it is God's intent and plan. Ephesians 6:17 refers to the written word and states, *"The sword of the Spirit, which is the word of God."* The psalmist wrote, *"I will worship toward thy holy temple, and praise thy name for thy lovingkindness and for thy truth: for thou hast magnified thy word above all thy name"* (Psalms 138:2). If there is any doubt that Christ fulfilled all of God's determinations, let him read: *"And he was clothed with a vesture dipped in blood: and his name is called The Word of God"* (Revelation 19:13).

REGARDING THE SAINTS: *"Then they that feared the Lord spake often one to another: and the Lord hearkened, and heard it, and a book of remembrance was written before him for them that feared the Lord, and that thought upon his name"* (Malachi 3:16). Included in the *"book,"* as shown in this Scripture, are the names and prayers of the saints. They are written in oneness with the Lamb slain from the foundation of the world. Christ's death was the deciding judgment factor and it is seconded by the death of the saints: *"Precious in the sight of the Lord is the death of his saints"* (Psalms 116:15). This is brought to bear and justifies God's judgment. *"And the smoke of the incense, which came with the prayers of the saints, ascended up before God out of the angel's hand"* (Revelation 8:4).

SEVEN SEALS: *"And I saw in the right hand of him that sat on the throne a book written within and on the backside, sealed with seven seals"* (Revelation 5:1). The first mention of a sealing pertaining to the vision was *"Seal up the vision"* (Daniel 9:24). Jesus fulfilled all prophecy, justifying the restitution, restoration, and continuance of creature and creation. Christ's sacrifice justified and initiated the at-one-ment of the Creator and mankind. At his death on the cross he said, *"It is finished"* (John 19:30). The revealing of the mystery of Christ and the *"restitution of all things"* is for and because of Jesus' love and obedience to his Father. Paul stated, *"For it pleased the Father that in him should all fullness dwell"* (Colossians 1:19). Daniel's mention, Daniel 9:24, *"seal up the vision"* relates directly to the "seven seals" of Revelation 5:1. Without controversy, Jesus is *"worthy to open the book, and to loose the seals thereof"* (Revelation 5:2). The seals were the keeping back of things to be made plain at the time of God's choosing. The opening of the *"book"* of God's intent, plan, and purpose, requires that the seals be loosed. The seals pertain to God's will, his declarations, and his mandates proceeded from the Holiest spirit realm. From the onset of the loosing of the seals, John *"heard, as it were the noise of thunder, one of the four beasts saying, Come and see"* (Revelation 6:1). The first four seals' openings were orchestrated by the four beasts stationed *"in the midst of the throne, and round about the throne"* (Revelation 4:6). Again, we note: If the twenty-four elders reflect the disposition of the 'Law' and the forgiveness of 'committed sin,' then the four living creatures reflect Christ, the dispensing of 'Grace,' with the forgiveness of 'original sin.' That was the freedom from the servitude of sin and death. That 'Spirit' provision was initiated with the price paid of Christ's shed blood. Jesus was that sacrifice which gained at-one-ment; our unifying of Spirit-spirit with God.

It is from God's throne that the mandates go forth, with those judgments being the declarations of the Latter Rain church. And, that opening, or dispensing, includes the headship of Christ and the officiation of the Archaeon Angels. That touches the interface of the heavenly and the earthly. In Revelation 11:4, it states, *"These are the two olive trees, and the two candlesticks standing before the God of the earth."* Without detail, we can say it shows the more complete order of God was witness to the martyrdom of the saints. The Church, of which Christ is the head, is submitted to that order. Paul brought this point of order to bear when he stated *"For this cause ought the women to have power on her head because of the angels"* (I Corinthians 11:10).

REFRESHING A PREVIOUS MENTION, WITH ADDED DETAIL: The temple is heaven's embodiment of God's plan. That plan is God's *"Word"* and *"intent"* toward the *"restitution of all things."* It was declared by the apostle Paul's statement in Galatians 4:26, *"But Jerusalem which is above is free, which is the mother of us all."* So being: *"Jerusalem which is above,"* is presently a unity with the *"temple of my God"* in heaven. In the finality *"that great city, the holy Jerusalem, descending* (descends) *out of heaven from God"* (Revelation 21:10). This equates to *"whom the heaven must receive until the times of restitution of all things"* (Acts 3:21). That is, Christ *"finished,"* price paid, thus realizing the plan of redemption and restitution. When that happens, God and the 'manifest God,' which is Christ, will reside with man. *"The tabernacle of God is with men, and he will dwell with them, and they shall be his people, and God himself shall be with them, and be their God"* (Revelation 21:3). Scriptures give further glorious report: *"And I saw no temple therein for the Lord God Almighty and the Lamb are the temple of it. And the city had no need of the sun, neither of the moon, to shine in it: for the glory of God did lighten it, and the Lamb is the light thereof"* (Revelation 21:22–23). That hope was given earlier to the church in Philadelphia. *"Him that overcometh will I make a pillar in the temple of my God, and he shall go no more out: and I will write upon him the name of my God, and the name of the city of my God, which is new Jerusalem, which cometh down out of heaven from my God: and I will write upon him my new name"* (Revelation 3:12).

Our calling is obedience to the heavenly vision, embraced by the Church Body, of which Jesus is the head. And, the Church is at-one-ment with the temple in heaven. That resides in the fact that we are rightly connected to God's plan in the Spirit-spirit connection. *"But he that is joined unto the Lord is one spirit"* (I Corinthians 6:17). Also, *"The Spirit itself beareth witness with our spirit that we are the children of God"* (Romans 8:16).

Further addressing the heavenly connection, Psalms 97:2 said, *"Righteousness and judgment are the habitation of his throne."* It is a certainty that his house, of which Christ is the cornerstone, is built according to *"Judgment also will I lay to the line, and righteousness to the plummet"* (Isaiah 28:17).

Refreshing the thought with some added detail: The temple in heaven is a sanctuary inclusive of God's throne and it is the habitation of God. It is his *"Word."* The temple-plan proceeds forward from there as God's will determines. While we confess that God is Spirit and permeates all the universe, we can see the temple as the plan or essence of his setting forth in the restitution and restoration of all things. Galatians 4:26 states, *"But Jerusalem which is above is free, which is the mother of us all."* John the revelator saw *"that great city, the holy Jerusalem, descending out of heaven from God"* (Revelation 21:10). The final 'rest' is realized when the temple is manifest as Jesus Christ; residing in the *"new heaven and a new earth"* (Revelation 21:1). Again; *"And I saw no temple therein: for the Lord God Almighty and the Lamb are the temple of it"* (Revelation 21:22). Again, *"And when all things shall be subdued unto him, then shall the Son also himself be subject unto him that put all things under him, that God may be all in all"* (I Corinthians 15:28). The "temple" speaks of the heavenly vision: God's plan and intent. Eternal past and eternal future, the *"Word"* resides with *"him that sat on the throne"* (Revelation 5:1): Our Lord and Savior Jesus Christ.

SEVEN THUNDERS, SEVEN VIALS, AND SEVEN PLAGUES: *"Seven thunders uttered their voices. And when the seven thunders had uttered their voices, I was about to write: and I heard a voice from heaven saying unto me, Seal up those things which the seven thunders uttered, and write them not"* (Revelation 10:3–4). This is the statement of God's determination. Later in the book of Revelation; *"And I saw another sign in heaven, great and marvelous, seven angels having the seven last plagues: for in them is filled up the wrath of God"* (Revelation 15:1). This can be seen as the going-forth decree. Later, the revealing of the seven thunders was allowed. And, it was spoken: *"And I heard a great voice out of the temple saying to the seven angels, Go your ways, and pour out the vials of the wrath of God upon the earth"* (Revelation 16:1). Thereafter, in this sixteenth chapter, the vials were poured out and the gathering for Armageddon was realized. The seventh vial of the seven was the 'event' of the war. That war was more God's wrath than the implementing of man's war machinery. The accomplishing of the thing was in the *"he gathered them together into a place called in the Hebrew tongue Armageddon. And the seventh angel poured out his vial into the air, and there came a great voice out of the temple of heaven, from the throne, saying, It is done"* (Revelation 16:16–17). John gave a direct statement of God's intent and the result. Going forward: *"And there came one of the seven angels which had the seven vials"* (Revelation 17:1), thus, the matter of God's judgment was made known to John for the record. So being, all mankind will know God's justice and the accomplishing of his judgments.

The plagues and vials are issued forth, thundered, *"upon the earth."* These are the phenomena or events applied to the time of the seventh seal; the final seal opening. That is: Seven thunders sounding seven vials of plagues poured into the earth. They are termed *vials and thunders* because there is no savor in these judgments; 'salt, having no savor.' Only God's voice of judgment unto destruction. No mediation. Again, seven thunders revealing the seven vials poured into the earth. It is the third woe. Repeating: It is the seventh seal/third woe. The seventh is sevenfold; seven thunders announcing seven vials poured out; seven plagues into the earth.

THE TRIUNE FACTOR, RELATING TO REALMS: First: God-Spirit realm is all-encompassing, and it is infinite, and it is timeless. God is Spirit and occupies all thought, space, and time. Touching his relationship with his creation and creatures, as shown by the tabernacle, is the 'Holiest.' *"One God and Father of all, who is above all, and through all, and in you all"* (Ephesians 4:6). Second: The earthly reflection: The psychological realm of thought/reasoning, and will and emotion. This realm is God-given and it is man's gift from God; God-given creativity and the innate ability, freedom, to act willfully. As per: *"And God said, Let us make man in our image, after our likeness"* (Genesis 1:26). As in-order and blessed, it is a 'Holy Place.' It is mandated to be the voice of God on earth. Third: The material, physical realm. This realm accommodates the observable creation, giving sustenance to life-forms; animate and inanimate. It can be likened to the 'Courts.'

CONCERNING RIGHTEOUSNESS: The triune factor relating to the collective and the individual. First: God is Spirit and man has been gifted the life of his Spirit. Second: Man is a manifest soul, psyche, person. Third: The body of the individual person. The third mention can include civilizations embodying man's six-thousand-year history; being *"peoples, and multitudes, and nations, and tongues"* (Revelation 17:15).

Man's godlikeness capacity, in his blessed estate, was to have the innate God-connection. One: Sensitivity of conscience toward God-Spirit realm. Two: Communion with God-Spirit realm. Three: Dominion as per the auspice of the God-Spirit realm connection.

The Creator-creature communion is the original anointing strengthening the inner man. God's predetermination is that the heaven-earth, and Creator-creature, and the Spirit-spirit unities be restored. Peace on earth. No more enmity. That is his will. When Jesus told his disciples how to pray, he stated, *"Our Father which art in heaven, Hallowed be thy name. Thy kingdom come, Thy will be done in earth, as it is in heaven"* (Matthew 6:9–10). God has ordained that we entertain the 'heavenly vision.' *"Eye hath not seen, nor ear heard, neither have entered into the heart of man, the things which God hath prepared for them that love him. But God hath revealed them unto us by his Spirit: for the Spirit searcheth all things, yea, the deep things of God"* (I Corinthians 2:9, 10). Our admonition: *"Fear God, and give glory to him; for the hour of his judgment is come: and worship him that made heaven, and earth, and the sea, and the fountains of waters"* (Revelation 14:7).

CONCERNING EVIL: Evil is empowered on three levels or three realms. That relates to three principals: Revelation 16:13 is a fitting Scripture depicting that fact. To wit: *"And I saw three unclean spirits like frogs come out of the mouth of the dragon, and out of the mouth of the beast, and out of the mouth of the false prophet"* (Revelation 16:13).

"The dragon": The imposition is *"a mark in their foreheads.* Having the "foreheads" unity, or mark, is to have an affinity of spirit with the dragon. This level of collusion is tantamount to being possessed of the devil. It is driven by the 'pride of life.' (The civil powers will totally register, unify, and integrate with the Adversary, Satan, the Devil. At that juncture, the Dragon is Satan's reflection, and the civil powers are correctly termed "d*ragon."*)

"The beast": The imposition is *"the number of his name."* That equates to a complicity with the system or body of evil. That being, *"peoples, and multitudes, and nations, and tongues"* (Revelation 17:15). To wit: Civilizations embodying man's six-thousand-year tenure. A compliance that gains you the continuance of the natural physical existence and bodily needs. It is driven by the 'lust of the flesh.'

"The false prophet": The imposition is *"a mark in their right hand."* That is to be in a right-hand fellowship with evil, being agreeable with the false voice and adopting the mind, will, and emotion of his message. On that psyche, soul level, you are onboard with the false prophet. The driving force is 'the lust of the eye.'

"Here is wisdom. Let him that hath understanding count the number of the beast: for it is the number of a man; and his number is Six hundred threescore and six" (Revelation 13:16–18). To wit: Spirit: The 'Dragon-man' operation is a six. The beast-man operation is a six. The false prophet-man operation is a six. Without the God-connection there is no godlikeness; just a natural beast. Paul, in his pastoral admonition, prayed for a seven, completeness, for the saints of Thessalonica. *"And the very God of peace sanctify you wholly; and I pray God your whole spirit and soul and body be preserved blameless unto the coming of our Lord Jesus Christ"* (I Thessalonians 5:23).

REFRESHING THE CONCEPT REGARDING THE THREE REALMS: First: The highest, where God's will emanate forth; the blue realm. It is from thence that heaven speaks God's *"intent."* It is God's realm or habitation. If the term *'abode'* was used in the Revelation text, it would be *"tabernacle."* Understood to be God's *"habitation,"* and therein is his *"righteousness and judgment"* (Psalms 96:2). The *"tabernacle"* is his house, his plan, his *"intent,"* and his *"Word."* Galatians 4:26 states it thus: *"Jerusalem which is above is free, which is the mother of us all."* In the restoration, it is described as *"the holy Jerusalem, descending out of heaven from God"* (Revelation 21:10); the 'theocratic kingdom,' being the new heaven and the new earth. *"Behold, the tabernacle of God is with men, and he will dwell with them, and they shall be his people, And God himself shall be with them, and be their God"* (Revelation 21:3). Second: The realm of God's will be done on earth. This is that estate where the Spirit-spirit connection exists and the Spirit leads man's spirit. This realm, God's order-in-the-earth, is a mystery. Embodying the Church, it is a heaven-in-the-earth operation. It is truly an 'in the world but not of the world' operation. The Spirit-spirit covering/realm reflects purple. We envision it as a tree with its roots in heaven. Per similitude, blue and red combine to produce purple. That exists when two are in unity. Jesus stated the principle; *"That they all may be one; as thou, Father, art in me, and I in thee, that they also may be one in us: that the world may believe that thou hast sent me"* (John 17:21). Third: The realm often referred to as the *'world.'* When reflecting the failed or fallen part, it is referred to as *"the first heaven and first earth."* It is centered on materialism and fleshly mandates. It is the earth and its' civilizations. However, like the body, "soma," definitively, it may be either good or evil. If tending to evil, it would be adversarial and against God; the 'unmitigated' first heaven red realm. The first heaven, when done away, leaves only the new heaven and new earth.

THE TABERNACLE OF MOSES IS A SIMILITUDE. It is *"a shadow of things to come,"* and reveals certain features of the three realms. Entering the tabernacle from the east and moving west, you enter the 'courts.' The 'Court' shows us the earth, our natural abode, and the brazen altar as dying to the world and the flesh. Then forward to the laver and *"that he might sanctify and cleanse it with the washing of water by the word"* (Ephesians 5:26). At that juncture, figuratively, you have 'cut your foot off.' A new walk. Thence forward, your works are no longer 'Adamic' and of the world. Figuratively, you cut your hand off. Leaving the works of the flesh behind, you move into the 'vision.' It is the covered tent of the tabernacle. Here your new life 'in Christ's will be brought forth. Figuratively, you have plucked your eye out; new light, new vision. The estate of "in the world but not of the world." Third is the realm of the 'Holiest,' and it is the Spirit drawing of God's Grace: "No man cometh to me except my father draw him." The Tabernacle of Moses pattern is foundational, depicting the plan of salvation on earth.

Restating the premise: Moving from 'a shadow of things to come,' we touch on Revelation's Spirit realm tabernacle; God's plan and intent. It is, as Paul stated in Galatians 4:26, *"the mother of us all."* It will be revealed, coming down from heaven and abiding preeminent on earth among the new earth dwellers. That is the gist of Revelation 21;2–3: *"And I John saw the holy city, new Jerusalem, coming down from God out of heaven, prepared as a bride adorned for her husband. And I heard a great voice out of heaven saying, Behold, the tabernacle of God is with men, and he will dwell with them, and they shall be his people, and God himself shall be with them, and be their God."*

CHAPTER IV
THE REVELATION

OPENING THE BOOK OF REVELATION: God speaks to mankind through prophecy, as per *"holy men of God spake as they were moved by the Holy Ghost"* (II Peter 1:21). Included also is the instrumentality of the Archaeon Angels, Gabriel and Michael. Such was the case with Moses at the burning bush. Michael was primary in the Old Testament dispensation. Daniel spoke of his role, toward the Jews as, *". . . the great prince which standeth for the children of thy people"* (Daniel 12:2). Michael continues, future, as a principal angel. *"And there was war in heaven; Michael and his angels fought against the dragon; and the dragon fought and his angels"* (Revelation 12:7).

New Testament Scriptures show Gabriel as the primary angel of the New Testament's declarations and dispensing. Third heaven angels have their mandated assignments and dispatches. Such was the case among mankind, where Paul's ministry was *"mighty in me"* toward the Gentiles. Peter *"wrought effectually"* toward the Jews. Both in heaven and on earth; one instrument in God's hand. The similitude: One beaten piece of gold.

The revealing of God's end-plan will be orchestrated by its author. Both angels and Spirit-led saints of God will accomplish the mandate. Much in the fashion of Paul's statement: *"Now then we are ambassadors for Christ, as though God did beseech you by us: we pray you in Christ's stead, be ye reconciled to God"* (II Corinthians 5:20). The initial giving of the Revelation unto Christ required no intermediary. By inheritance and then as being the atonement, Jesus is both *"the author and finisher of our faith"* (Hebrews 12:2). Consider: Christ was *"by the right hand of God exalted"* (Acts 2:33), so that he was integral to the highest heavenly order and totally integrated into the inner sanctum of the Almighty God. God's plan for the *"restitution of all things"* sees Christ as preeminent. Christ was a reality and abode with God from the beginning and yet to be revealed prophesied-Christ, God's *"Word."* He abode as God's hidden wisdom, eternal and omnipresent. To the discerning heart, Jesus is the *"alpha and omega"* of both the Revelation and our salvation. However perceived, the dispensing of the Revelation was glorious and beyond human expression. We confess, and we suborn, to the Lord God. We *"stand in awe and sin not."* The Revelation required no intermediary between God and his Son.

The conveyance of the knowledge and wisdom of Revelation is Christ's right to dispense to mankind. The knowledge of the nearing event of that dispensing is the burden of this writing. The dispensing of the truth of Revelation is time-sensitive. *"Dispensation,"* as relates to the end-time ordination of the Church is primary. The wisdom of the dispensing will be flavored with humility and sacrifice.

As per the 'orders' of a Holy Ghost operation, Christ conveyed the message by the instrumentality of *"his angel"* to John. That angel may have been an Archaeon Angel. However, reading into the book of Revelation and noting the interaction of John with the angel, we are led to think that the angel was Daniel. His appearing to John would be in a like manner as Moses and Elijah appeared to Jesus on the Mount of Transfiguration. This may give pause to the reader, but I believe such was the case when Samuel appeared to Saul in the record of I Samuel 28:7–20.

These beginning statements regarding Revelation are helpful, even necessary, in further understanding and our confession that God's predeterminations are given to mankind because of His giving and then the dispensing of Christ from heaven, Jesus' life and his death on the cross. Because of that dispensing of the atonement, we are granted the pathway to knowing spiritual things. Again, the revealing of Revelation's God-ordained truth is 'dispensational.' The declarations of Revelation mysteries are being delegated, in a timely manner, to God-ordained officiation and made known to his cloud of final, second witnesses.

A point of understanding: The phrase *'because of'*, used above, equates to *"by him,"* as stated in Scripture. *"For by him were all things created, that are in heaven, and that are in earth, visible and invisible, whether they be thrones, or dominions, or principalities, or powers: all things were created by him, and for him: And he is before all things, and by him all things consist"* (Colossians 1:16, 17). That fact of God's plan is clearly stated: *"For it pleased the Father that in him should all fullness dwell;* to wit: *"For in him dwelleth all the fullness of the Godhead bodily"* (Colossians 1:19, 2:9). Reasonably, God's *"Word"* and *"intent"* predated the advent of the things that were prophesied.

CHAPTER V

REVELATION, CHAPTERS 1-3

CHAPTERS 1 THROUGH 3 are given without deletions. The reader is encouraged to read the chapters without omissions. The accompanying commentary, however abbreviated, is meant to help the reader understand the message.

CHAPTER 1: *1. "The Revelation of Jesus Christ, which God gave unto him, to shew unto his servants things which must shortly come to pass; and he sent and signified it by his angel unto his servant John: 2. Who bare record of the word of God, and of the testimony of Jesus Christ, and of all things that he saw. 3. Blessed is he that readeth, and they that hear the words of this prophecy, and keep those things which are written therein: for the time is at hand. 4. John to the seven churches which are in Asia: Grace be unto you, and peace, from him which is, and which was, and which is to come; and from the seven Spirits which are before his throne; 5. And from Jesus Christ, who is the faithful witness, and the first begotten of the dead, and the prince of the kings of the earth. Unto him that loved us, and washed us from our sins in his own blood, 6. And hath made us kings and priests unto God and his Father; to him be glory and dominion for ever and ever. Amen. 7. Behold, he cometh with clouds; and every eye shall see him, and they also which pierced him: and all kindreds of the earth shall wail because of him. Even so, Amen. 8. I am Alpha and Omega, the beginning and the ending, saith the Lord, which is, and which was, and which is to come, the Almighty. 9. I John, who also am your brother, and companion in tribulation, and in the kingdom and patience of Jesus Christ, was in the isle that is called Patmos, for the word of God, and for the testimony of Jesus Christ. 10. I was in the Spirit on the Lord's day, and heard behind me a great voice, as of a trumpet, 11. Saying, I am Alpha and Omega, the first and the last: and, What thou seest, write in a book, and send it unto the seven churches which are in Asia; unto Ephesus, and unto Smyrna, and unto Pergamos, and unto Thyatira, and unto Sardis, and unto Philadelphia, and unto Laodicea. 12. And I turned to see the voice that spake with me. And being turned, I saw seven golden candlesticks; 13. And in the midst of the seven candlesticks one like unto the Son of man, clothed with a garment down to the foot, and girt about the paps with a golden girdle. 14. His head and his hairs were white like wool, as white as snow; and his eyes were as a flame of fire; 15. And his feet like unto fine brass, as if they burned in a furnace; and his voice as the sound of many waters. 16. And he had in his right hand seven stars: and out of his mouth went a sharp twoedged sword: and his countenance was as the sun shineth in his strength. 17. And when I saw him, I fell at his feet as dead. And he laid his right hand upon me, saying unto me, Fear not; I am the first and the last: 18. I am he that liveth, and was dead; and, behold, I am alive for evermore, Amen; and have the keys of hell and of death. 19. Write the things which thou hast seen, and the things which are, and the things which shall be hereafter; 20. The mystery of the seven stars which thou sawest in my right hand, and the seven golden candlesticks. The seven stars are the angels of the seven churches: and the seven candlesticks which thou sawest are the seven churches."*

John is mandated to write to the saints, being in the world but not of the world. Regarding the audience, the statement was explicit: *"For the time is at hand."*

VERSES 1–3: *1. "The Revelation of Jesus Christ, which God gave unto him, to shew unto his servants things which must shortly come to pass; and he sent and signified it by his angel unto his servant John: 2. Who bare record of the word of God, and of the testimony of Jesus Christ, and of all things that he saw. 3. Blessed is he that readeth, and they that hear the words of this prophecy, and keep those things which are written therein: for the time is at hand."*

The revelation of Jesus Christ is both possessive and definitive. Possessive in the sense of Christ being both the embodiment and the revealing of God's *"Word."* He is *"heir of all things, by whom also he made the worlds"* (Hebrews 1:2). Also, simply stated, *"And ye are Christ's and Christ is God's"* (I Corinthians 3:23). It is definitive in the sense that Christ was the revealing of God's *"intent"* which is given to Christ for his right to reveal the Revelation to *"his servants."*

The statements *"which must shortly come to pass"* and *"for the time is at hand,"* apply to Revelation chapters 2 and 3. In that regard, we note that chapter 4 begins *"things which must be hereafter."* The text states that God *"sent and signified it by his angel unto his servant John."* Reasonably, that angel could be Gabriel, Archaeon Angel, as per ministering or mediating the advent of Christ' coming; born of a virgin. Christ himself could have manifest as *"his angel"* as 'prophet status' and separated from the Revelation vision. Other passages, namely Revelation 19:10 and 22:9, indicate a status of *"fellow servant, and of thy brethren."* That statement, in context, indicates a 'resurrection phenomenon,' in the like fashion of Elijah and Moses appearing to Christ on the mount and Samuel appearing to Saul on the day of his death. That thought allows the possibility that *"his angel"* was the prophet Daniel.

VERSES 4–8: *4. "John to the seven churches which are in Asia: Grace be unto you, and peace, from him which is, and which was, and which is to come; and from the seven Spirits which are before his throne; 5. And from Jesus Christ, who is the faithful witness, and the first begotten of the dead, and the prince of the kings of the earth. Unto him that loved us, and washed us from our sins in his own blood, 6. And hath made us kings and priests unto God and his Father; to him be glory and dominion for ever and ever. Amen. 7. Behold, he cometh with clouds; and every eye shall see him, and they also which pierced him: and all kindreds of the earth shall wail because of him. Even so, Amen. 8. I am Alpha and Omega, the beginning and the ending, saith the Lord, which is, and which was, and which is to come, the Almighty."*

John wonderfully identifies Jesus and then directs that glory and station toward loving and keeping and glorifying the Church and the saints. Regarding *"the seven Spirits which are before his throne:"* The candlestick positioned in the Holy Place is a similitude. The candlestick, center branch, is Christ and the six branches, as paired in the text, would be wisdom-understanding, counsel-might, and knowledge-fear of the Lord. Furthermore, in the above-quoted verse 5, he is described as *"faithful witness, first begotten of the dead and prince of the kings of the earth."* Beyond his innate godliness, we read what that means in terms of his love and gift to his beloved children. This similitude is a unity relating to the four living creatures; Jesus is the Lion of the tribe of Judah, he is sacrificial, he is sinless man, and he is Divinity as our Risen Savior.

VERSES 9–11: *9. "I John, who also am your brother, and companion in tribulation, and in the kingdom and patience of Jesus Christ, was in the isle that is called Patmos, for the word of God, and for the testimony of Jesus Christ. 10. I was in the Spirit on the Lord's day, and heard behind me a great voice, as of a trumpet, 11. Saying, I am Alpha and Omega, the first and the last: and, What thou seest, write in a book, and send it unto the seven churches which are in Asia; unto Ephesus, and unto Smyrna, and unto Pergamos, and unto Thyatira, and unto Sardis, and unto Philadelphia, and unto Laodicea."*

John identifies himself, his mandate, and his strait. The conversation graduates to *"I was in the Spirit on the Lord's Day."* The voice was *"as a trumpet."* Typically, that sound proceeded from the Highest Realm. The *"Alpha and Omega, the first and the last"* commissions John to write the vision and send it to the seven churches. The text leaves no doubt that these were seven existing, viable, churches.

VERSES 12–20: *12. "And I turned to see the voice that spake with me. And being turned, I saw seven golden candlesticks; 13. And in the midst of the seven candlesticks one like unto the Son of man, clothed with a garment down to the foot, and girt about the paps with a golden girdle. 14. His head and his hairs were white like wool, as white as snow; and his eyes were as a flame of fire; 15. And his feet like unto fine brass, as if they burned in a furnace; and his voice as the sound of many waters. 16. And he had in his right hand seven stars: and out of his mouth went a sharp twoedged sword: and his countenance was as the sun shineth in his strength. 17. And when I saw him, I fell at his feet as dead. And he laid his right hand upon me, saying unto me, Fear not; I am the first and the last: 18. I am he that liveth, and was dead; and, behold, I am alive for evermore, Amen; and have the keys of hell and of death. 19. Write the things which thou hast seen, and the things which are, and the things which shall be hereafter; 20. The mystery of the seven stars which thou sawest in my right hand, and the seven golden candlesticks. The seven stars are the angels of the seven churches: and the seven candlesticks which thou sawest are the seven churches."*

Paul, giving his like-experience, stated *"whether in the body, or out of the body, I cannot tell"* (II Corinthians 12:3). John's experience was different, in the sense that he knowingly *"turned to see the voice that spake with me."* The portrayal of Christ, godlike, is given in several glorious likenesses. In the next two chapters, those divine portrayals are given singularly to each of the churches. This chapter concludes with John giving the *"mystery of the seven stars . . . and the seven candlesticks."* The understanding of *"mystery"* includes the principal of 'twofold.' Calling on a 'similitude' for clarification: The seven candlesticks, churches, are a "Holy Place" operation and does reflect Christ, who perfectly reflects the seven spirits of God. The *"angels of the seven churches"* are the visible Ministers of the Church; terrestrial. Present are celestial angels. *"Are they not all ministering spirits, sent forth to minister for them who shall be heirs of salvation?"* (Hebrews 1:14)

CHAPTER 2: *1. "Unto the angel of* **the church of Ephesus** *write; These things saith he that holdeth the seven stars in his right hand, who walketh in the midst of the seven golden candlesticks; 2. I know thy works, and thy labour, and thy patience, and how thou canst not bear them which are evil: and thou hast tried them which say they are apostles, and are not, and hast found them liars: 3. And hast borne, and hast patience, and for my name's sake hast laboured, and hast not fainted." 4. Nevertheless I have somewhat against thee, because thou* *hast left thy first love. 5. Remember therefore from whence thou art fallen, and repent, and do the first works; or else I will come unto thee quickly, and will remove thy candlestick out of his place, except thou repent. 6. But this thou hast, that thou hatest the deeds of the Nicolaitanes, which I also hate. 7. He that hath an ear, let him hear what the Spirit saith unto the churches; To him that overcometh will I give to eat of the tree of life, which is in the midst of the paradise of God. 8. "And unto the angel of* **the church** *in Smyrna write; These things saith the first and the last, which was dead, and is alive; 9. I know thy works, and tribulation, and poverty, (but thou art rich) and I know the blasphemy of them which say they are Jews, and are not, but are the synagogue of Satan. 10. Fear none of those things which thou shalt suffer: behold, the devil shall cast some of you into prison, that ye may be tried; and ye shall have tribulation ten days: be thou faithful unto death, and I will give thee a crown of life. 11. He that hath an ear, let him hear what the Spirit saith unto the churches; He that overcometh shall not be hurt of the second death. 12. And to the angel of* **the church in Pergamos** *write; These things saith he which hath the sharp sword with two edges; 13. I know thy works, and where thou dwellest, even where Satan's seat is: and thou holdest fast my name, and hast not denied my faith, even in those days wherein Antipas was my faithful martyr, who was slain among you, where Satan dwelleth. 14. But I have a few things against thee, because thou hast there them that hold the doctrine of Balaam, who taught Balac to cast a stumblingblock before the children of Israel, to eat things sacrificed unto idols, and to commit fornication. 15. So hast thou also them that hold the doctrine of the Nicolaitanes, which thing I hate. 16. Repent; or else I will come unto thee quickly, and will fight against them with the sword of my mouth. 17. He that hath an ear, let him hear what the Spirit saith unto the churches; To him that overcometh will I give to eat of the hidden manna, and will give him a white stone, and in the stone a new name written, which no man knoweth saving he that receiveth it. 18. And unto the angel of* **the church in Thyatira** *write; These things saith the Son of God, who hath his eyes like unto a flame of fire, and his feet are like fine brass; 19. I know thy works, and charity, and service, and faith, and thy patience, and thy works; and the last to be more than the first. 20. Notwithstanding I have a few things against thee, because thou sufferest that woman Jezebel, which calleth herself a prophetess, to teach and to seduce my servants to commit fornication, and to eat things sacrificed unto idols. 21. And I gave her space to repent of her fornication; and she repented not. 22. Behold, I will cast her into a bed, and them that commit adultery with her into great tribulation, except they repent of their deeds. 23. And I will kill her children with death; and all the churches shall know that I am he which searcheth the reins and hearts: and I will give unto every one of you according to your works. 24. But unto you I say, and unto the rest in Thyatira, as many as have not this doctrine, and which have not known the depths of Satan, as they speak; I will put upon you none other burden. 25. But that which ye have already hold fast till I come. 26. And he that overcometh, and keepeth my works unto the end, to him will I give power over the nations: 27. And he shall rule them with a rod of iron; as the vessels of a potter shall they be broken to shivers: even as I received of my Father. 28. And I will give him the morning star. 29. He that hath an ear, let him hear what the Spirit saith unto the churches."*

VERSES 1–3: *1. "Unto the angel of* **the church of Ephesus** *write; These things saith he that holdeth the seven stars in his right hand, who walketh in the midst of the seven golden candlesticks; 2. I know thy works, and thy labour, and thy patience, and how thou canst not bear them which are evil: and thou hast tried them which say they are apostles, and are not, and hast found them liars: 3. And hast borne, and hast patience, and for my name's sake hast laboured, and hast not fainted."*

The angel identifies himself as holding the star in his right hand. This reflects a good estate for the minister of the church. Patience is mentioned twice. That is a commendation in itself, and beyond that, their labor and integrity are commended. Knowing the burden of the church officers, it is evident that the work of the apostle is intact. *"Judgment to the line"* (Isaiah 28:17). That is, judgment, good order, doctrine, and proper treatment of offences toward the church.

VERSES 4–7: *4. "Nevertheless I have somewhat against thee, because thou hast left thy first love. 5. Remember therefore from whence thou art fallen, and repent, and do the first works; or else I will come unto thee quickly, and will remove thy candlestick out of his place, except thou repent. 6. But this thou hast, that thou hatest the deeds of the Nicolaitanes, which I also hate. 7. He that hath an ear, let him hear what the Spirit saith unto the churches; To him that overcometh will I give to eat of the tree of life, which is in the midst of the paradise of God."*

The event of receiving the Holy Ghost was our birth into the family of God. Included is the introduction of his love into our spirit. It is our first love and we must cherish that experience and keep it alive. It is the nature of Christ imputed to us. It is the nature and savor of our new man. We stand in awe, as born-again and gifted with God's love. *". . . The love of God is shed abroad in our hearts by the Holy Ghost which is given unto us"* (Romans 5:5). *". . . Thy first love"* (Revelation 2:4). *"For God so loved the world, that he gave his only begotten Son, that whosoever believeth in him should not perish, but have everlasting life"* (John 3:16). I Corinthians 13:13 states, *"And now abideth faith, hope, charity, these three; but the greatest of these is charity."* We must know experientially that God's love is foundational. And, we have tasted that 'higher ground' in our personal Spirit-spirit conversion experience. Let us never leave that *"first love."* Leaving their *"first love"* equated to leaving the foundation of their faith. Tragedy it is, if our circumcision becomes uncircumcision; loss of sensitivity of conscience that comes with circumcision. An outstanding emotion that comes with the Holy Ghost experience is LOVE. We love even our enemies. Conversion and Holy Ghost baptism experiences are ongoing. That must not pass away, being the imputed righteousness of Christ; as per *"that we might be made the righteousness of God in him"* (II Corinthians 5:21). We know it to be the heavenly connection; Church is so positioned, *"righteousness to the plummet"* (Isaiah 28:17). That relates to the office of the Prophet. Without Jesus' advent, that foundational part was wanting. *"For the testimony of Jesus is the spirit of prophecy"* (Revelation 19:10). Having the testimony of Jesus is to have the love of God indwelling us. Let us hear the admonition to the Church, lest we leave our first love. That earmark would be to entertain an unforgiving spirit in the face of Christ pardoning our death sentence; denying the atonement.

VERSES 8–11: *8. "And unto the angel of* **the church in Smyrna** *write; These things saith the first and the last, which was dead, and is alive; 9. I know thy works, and tribulation, and poverty, (but thou art rich) and I know the blasphemy of them which say they are Jews, and are not, but are the synagogue of Satan. 10. Fear none of those things which thou shalt suffer: behold, the devil shall cast some of you into prison, that ye may be tried; and ye shall have tribulation ten days: be thou faithful unto death, and I will give thee a crown of life. 11. He that hath an ear, let him hear what the Spirit saith unto the churches; He that overcometh shall not be hurt of the second death."*

The angel of the church portrayed victory over death. As per James 2:5, *"Harken, my beloved brethren, Hath not God chosen the poor of this world rich in faith, and heirs of the kingdom which he hath promised to them that love him?"* In terms of tribulation, the church was *"rich in faith."* Their poverty was noteworthy. A point in question: Concerning the church in Laodicea, it was stated, *"Because thou sayest, I am rich, and increased with goods, and have need of nothing; and knowest not that thou art wretched, and miserable, and poor, and blind, and naked"* (Revelation 3:17). The term *"rich,"* in a condemning sense toward Laodicea, does not apply to the church in Smyrna. Again; the statement *"but thou art rich"* should be taken as rich in the things of God. That being the case, this church was not cited for any wrongdoing. Their hope was in the fact of their resurrection promise; a *"crown of life."* The church in Ephesus was guilty of leaving their first love. They were in danger of forfeiting life in resurrection. By contrast, the church in Smyrna had laid hold of eternal life in Christ.

VERSES 12–13: *12. "And to the angel of* **the church in Pergamos** *write; These things saith he which hath the sharp sword with two edges; 13. I know thy works, and where thou dwellest, even where Satan's seat is: and thou holdest fast my name, and hast not denied my faith, even in those days wherein Antipas was my faithful martyr, who was slain among you, where Satan dwelleth."*

The angel of the church was strong in the word and the rule of God. The church is strong in works and in faith.

VERSES 14–17: *14. "But I have a few things against thee, because thou hast there them that hold the doctrine of Balaam, who taught Balac to cast a stumblingblock before the children of Israel, to eat things sacrificed unto idols, and to commit fornication. 15. So hast thou also them that hold the doctrine of the Nicolaitanes, which thing I hate. 16. Repent; or else I will come unto thee quickly, and will fight against them with the sword of my mouth. 17. He that hath an ear, let him hear what the Spirit saith unto the churches; To him that overcometh will I give to eat of the hidden manna, and will give him a white stone, and in the stone a new name written, which no man knoweth saving he that receiveth it."*

This church was situated in an evil community. Apparently, evil was allowed to abide in the camp. The core of the church may have been committed, but there was a liberality in the ruling rank that did not see the need to purge the camp. That same allowance cost Israel its purity in the days of Balaam and Balac. The price of the *"fight against them"* would be to devastate the societal landscape. Resisting sin from entering the sanctuary is difficult to maintain, but cleansing the sin abiding within the sanctuary often requires a total disassembly and restart.

VERSE 18–19: *18. "And unto the angel of* **the church in Thyatira** *write; These things saith the Son of God, who hath his eyes like unto a flame of fire, and his feet are like fine brass; 19. I know thy works, and charity, and service, and faith, and thy patience, and thy works; and the last to be more than the first."*

The angel of the church was portrayed as strong in declaring the message and vision of the 'furnace of affliction.' The church excelled in 'works.'

VERSES 20–29: *20. "Notwithstanding I have a few things against thee, because thou sufferest that woman Jezebel, which calleth herself a prophetess, to teach and to seduce my servants to commit fornication, and to eat things sacrificed unto idols. 21. And I gave her space to repent of her fornication; and she repented not. 22. Behold, I will cast her into a bed, and them that commit adultery with her into great tribulation, except they repent of their deeds. 23. And I will kill her children with death; and all the churches shall know that I am he which searcheth the reins and hearts: and I will give unto every one of you according to your works. 24. But unto you I say, and unto the rest in Thyatira, as many as have not this doctrine, and which have not known the depths of Satan, as they speak; I will put upon you none other burden. 25. But that which ye have already hold fast till I come. 26. And he that overcometh, and keepeth my works unto the end, to him will I give power over the nations: 27. And he shall rule them with a rod of iron; as the vessels of a potter shall they be broken to shivers: even as I received of my Father. 28. And I will give him the morning star. 29. He that hath an ear, let him hear what the Spirit saith unto the churches."*

The core principle of a *"Jezebel"* operation is the perversion of God's order. A perversion that puts witches over warlocks. Peculiar to perverted order is the literal perversion of natural things. The *"Jezebel"* mentality allows for an anything-goes mentality.

CHAPTER 3: *1. "And unto the angel of* **the church in Sardis** *write; These things saith he that hath the seven Spirits of God, and the seven stars; I know thy works, that thou hast a name that thou livest, and art dead. 2. Be watchful, and strengthen the things which remain, that are ready to die: for I have not found thy works perfect before God. 3. Remember therefore how thou hast received and heard, and hold fast, and repent. If therefore thou shalt not watch, I will come on thee as a thief, and thou shalt not know what hour I will come upon thee. 4. Thou hast a few names even in Sardis which have not defiled their garments; and they shall walk with me in white: for they are worthy." 5. "He that overcometh, the same shall be clothed in white raiment; and I will not blot out his name out of the book of life, but I will confess his name before my Father, and before his angels. 6. He that hath an ear, let him hear what the Spirit saith unto the churches. 7. And to the angel of* **the church in Philadelphia** *write; These things saith he that is holy, he that is true, he that hath the key of David, he that openeth, and no man shutteth; and shutteth, and no man openeth; 8. I know thy works: behold, I have set before thee an open door, and no man can shut it: for thou hast a little strength, and hast kept my word, and hast not denied my name. 9. Behold, I will make them of the synagogue of Satan, which say they are Jews, and are not, but do lie; behold, I will make them to come and worship before thy feet, and to know that I have loved thee. 10. Because thou hast kept the word of my patience, I also will keep thee from the hour of temptation, which shall come upon all the world, to try them that dwell upon the earth. 11. Behold, I come quickly: hold that fast which thou hast, that no man take thy crown. 12. Him that overcometh will I make a pillar in the temple of my God, and he shall go no more out: and I will write upon him the name of my God, and the name of the city of my God, which is new Jerusalem, which cometh down out of heaven from my God: and I will write upon him my new name. 13. He that hath an ear, let him hear what the Spirit saith unto the churches. 14. And unto the angel of* **the church of the Laodiceans** *write; These things saith the Amen, the faithful and true witness, the beginning of the creation of God; 15. I know thy works, that thou art neither cold nor hot: I would thou wert cold or hot. 16. So then because thou art lukewarm, and neither cold nor hot, I will spue thee out of my mouth. 17. Because thou sayest, I am rich, and increased with goods, and have need of nothing; and knowest not that thou art wretched, and miserable, and poor, and blind, and naked: 18. I counsel thee to buy of me gold tried in the fire, that thou mayest be rich; and white raiment, that thou mayest be clothed, and that the shame of thy nakedness do not appear; and anoint thine eyes with eyesalve, that thou mayest see. 19. As many as I love, I rebuke and chasten: be* zealous therefore, and repent. 20. Behold, I stand at the door, and knock: if any man hear my voice, and open the door, I will come in to him, and will sup with him, and he with me. 21. To him that overcometh will I grant to sit with me in my throne, even as I also overcame, and am set down with my Father in his throne. 22. He that hath an ear, let him hear what the Spirit saith unto the churches."

VERSES 1–6: *1. "And unto the angel of* **the church in Sardis** *write; These things saith he that hath the seven Spirits of God, and the seven stars; I know thy works, that thou hast a name that thou livest, and art dead. 2. Be watchful, and strengthen the things which remain, that are ready to die: for I have not found thy works perfect before God. 3. Remember therefore how thou hast received and heard, and hold fast, and repent. If therefore thou shalt not watch, I will come on thee as a thief, and thou shalt not know what hour I will come upon thee. 4. Thou hast a few names even in Sardis which have not defiled their garments; and they shall walk with me in white: for they are worthy. 5. He that overcometh, the same shall be clothed in white raiment; and I will not blot out his name out of the book of life, but I will confess his name before my Father, and before his angels. 6. He that hath an ear, let him hear what the Spirit saith unto the churches."*

The angel portrays the dispositional, spiritual part. He associates with the visible headship of the church. The final 'products' of the church are the overcomers. The message of dying to sin is foundational to the church and here that message is being challenged and weakened. The church ministry is encouraged to *"hold fast."* Jesus used this expression of *"watch."* Simply put, as per Strong's Dictionary, stay awake and be vigilant. His disciples went to sleep at a critical time, in the garden, while he was in agonizing prayer. Paul stated, *"And that, knowing the time, that now it is high time to awake out of sleep: for now is our salvation nearer than when we believed"* (Romans 13:11).

VERSES 7–13: *7. "And to the angel of* **the church in Philadelphia** *write; These things saith he that is holy, he that is true, he that hath the key of David, he that openeth, and no man shutteth; and shutteth, and no man openeth; 8. I know thy works: behold, I have set before thee an open door, and no man can shut it: for thou hast a little strength, and hast kept my word, and hast not denied my name. 9. behold, I will make them of the synagogue of Satan, which say they are Jews, and are not, but do lie; behold, I will make them to come and worship before thy feet, and to know that I have loved thee. 10. Because thou hast kept the word of my patience, I also will keep thee from the hour of temptation, which shall come upon all the world, to try them that dwell upon the earth. 11. Behold, I come quickly: hold that fast which thou hast, that no man take thy crown. 12. Him that overcometh will I make a pillar in the temple of my God, and he shall go no more out: and I will write upon him the name of my God, and the name of the city of my God, which is new Jerusalem, which cometh down out of heaven from my God: and I will write upon him my new name. 13. He that hath an ear, let him hear what the Spirit saith unto the churches."*

The Lord gives credit and blessing toward the Church. He is defensive and protective toward the Church. The reflections are good and to be desired.

VERSES 14–22: *14. "And unto the angel of* **the church of the Laodiceans** *write; These things saith the Amen, the faithful and true witness, the beginning of the creation of God; 15. I know thy works, that thou art neither cold nor hot: I would thou wert cold or hot. 16. So then because thou art lukewarm, and neither cold nor hot, I will spue thee out of my mouth. 17. Because thou sayest, I am rich, and increased with goods, and have* *need of nothing; and knowest not that thou art wretched, and miserable, and poor, and blind, and naked: 18. I counsel thee to buy of me gold tried in the fire, that thou mayest be rich; and white raiment, that thou mayest be clothed, and that the shame of thy nakedness do not appear; and anoint thine eyes with eyesalve, that thou mayest see. 19. As many as I love, I rebuke and chasten: be zealous therefore, and repent. 20. Behold, I stand at the door, and knock: if any man hear my voice, and open the door, I will come in to him, and will sup with him, and he with me. 21. To him that overcometh will I grant to sit with me in my throne, even as I also overcame, and am set down with my Father in his throne. 22. He that hath an ear, let him hear what the Spirit saith unto the churches."*

The angel was notably a *"faithful and true witness."* In heaven and on earth, that is foundational. This church may have been somewhat conformable to the message, but it was not *"zealous."* Their prescription for *"faithful and true"* may have been seasoned with apathy.

CHAPTER VI

REVELATION, CHAPTERS 4-5

REVELATION CHAPTERS 4 THROUGH 5 REFLECT THE THIRD HEAVEN. This 'Spirit realm' is the highest, and as per the tabernacle similitude, it is the 'Blue' Holiest compartment. To wit: The God-realm, from whence God reveals his will and intent; first, to Jesus Christ and, thence, by his angel, to John.

CHAPTER 4: *1. "After this I looked, and, behold, a door was opened in heaven: and the first voice which I heard was as it were of a trumpet talking with me; which said, Come up hither, and I will shew thee things which must be hereafter. 2. And immediately I was in the spirit: and, behold, a throne was set in heaven, and one sat on the throne. 3. And he that sat was to look upon like a jasper and a sardine stone: and there was a rainbow round about the throne, in sight like unto an emerald. 4. And round about the throne were four and twenty seats: and upon the seats I saw four and twenty elders sitting, clothed in white raiment; and they had on their heads crowns of gold. 5. And out of the throne proceeded lightnings and thunderings and voices: and there were seven lamps of fire burning before the throne, which are the seven Spirits of God. 6. And before the throne there was a sea of glass like unto crystal: and in the midst of the throne, and round about the throne, were four beasts full of eyes before and behind. 7. And the first beast was like a lion, and the second beast like a calf, and the third beast had a face as a man, and the fourth beast was like a flying eagle. 8. And the four beasts had each of them six wings about him; and they were full of eyes within: and they rest not day and night, saying, Holy, holy, holy, Lord God Almighty, which was, and is, and is to come. 9. And when those beasts give glory and honor and thanks to him that sat on the throne, who liveth for ever and ever, 10. The four and twenty elders fall down before him that sat on the throne, and worship him that liveth for ever and ever, and cast their crowns before the throne, saying, 11. Thou art worthy, O Lord, to receive glory and honor and power: for thou hast created all things, and for thy pleasure they are and were created."*

Heaven's glory and declarations are without regard to time.

The first word *"after,"* indicates a time break in the narrative. At this point, the time reference is taken to be future. The description *"a door was opened in heaven"* is literal relating to the vision. Beyond the literal observation, it leads the spiritual thinking mind to the confession that Jesus is the 'Door.' Jesus is the at-one-ment that allows even a limited vision of the Spirit realm. John hears a *"voice . . . as it were of a trumpet."* That terminology indicates a statement issued from the Spirit realm. Having been called, *"Come up hither,"* John first beheld *"a throne was set in heaven, and one sat on the throne."* The word *throne* is mentioned thirty-nine times in the book of Revelation. By definition, the seat of a potentate. Here, it is the Chair of Omnipotence.

We confess that God is omnipresent. Scripturewise, we go to Ephesians 4:6 for an akin statement: *"One God and Father of all, who is above all, and through all, and in you all."* In this revelation, God does act in a fashion as having a point of emanation. The *"throne"* would be that 'point' or focus and the seat or habitation of his *"Word."* That is, his plan and his *"intent"* toward his creation. Having mentioned the *"throne,"* two additional principals are mentioned: The *"temple"* and the *"tabernacle."* The understanding, however limited, will be helpful: The *"temple,"* later spoken of sixteen times, may be considered the heavenly dwelling or embodiment of his *"Word."* The *"temple"* is mentioned in connection with the *"tabernacle."* To wit: *"And after that I looked, and, behold, the temple of the tabernacle of the testimony in heaven was opened"* (Revelation 15:5). The *"tabernacle"* may be considered as the 'setting forth' of his *"Word,"* his plan, his *"intent."* Jesus is the atonement that made it possible. And, it will be 'finished.' *"And I heard a great voice out of heaven saying, Behold, the tabernacle of God is with men, and he will dwell with them, and they shall be his people, and God himself shall be with them, and be their God"* (Revelation 21:3). Again, being 'finished,' it is manifest in the new heaven and new earth. To wit: *"And I saw no temple therein: for the Lord God Almighty and the Lamb are the temple of it"* (Revelation 21:22).

Declarations from the third heaven realm are conveyed to mankind via the realm of compliant God-ordained officiation; the compliant intermediary's compartment. That blessed estate of the God-ordained, compliant officiation of the Church. So being, the Church facilitates the operation of God's will and intent on earth. Repeating: This realm can be termed the *intermediary realm; "in heavenly places in Christ"* (Ephesians 1:3). Jesus stated, *"They are not of the world, even as I am not of the world"* (John 17:16). Christ is the head of the Church. The head, Christ, is now in heaven and he was, and is, the personification of God's *"Word."* So being, Christ reveals God's plan and intent for his creation and creatures. And, the 'Body of Christ,' which is his Church, is heaven-connected; Spirit-spirit. Settlements of God's justice and judgments are thus made obvious in the realm of in-the-earth mankind. Both the believing and the unbelieving will be judged by those declarations. Some unto eternal life and some unto eternal damnation. As per the tabernacle similitude, this earthly realm is where God's judgment is accomplished. Going forward, Revelation gives us a description of the Spirit-God's plan of the ages. The voice is as a trumpet and it required that John be elevated to *"in the spirit."* To wit:

VERSES 1–3: *1. "After this I looked, and behold, a door was opened in heaven: and the first voice which I heard was as it were of a trumpet talking with me; which said, come up hither, and I will shew thee things which must be hereafter. 2. And immediately I was in the spirit; and behold, a throne was set in heaven, and one sat on the throne. 3. And he that sat was to look upon like a jasper and a sardine stone: and there was a rainbow round about the throne, in sight like unto an emerald."*

Ephesians 4:6 states it thus: *"One God and Father of all, who is above all, and through all, and in you all."*

TWENTY-FOUR ELDERS

VERSE 4: *"And round about the throne were four and twenty seats: and upon the seats I saw four and twenty elders sitting, clothed in white raiment; and they had on their heads crowns of gold."* The last verses of the chapter portray these twenty-four elders as actual entities. They worshipped God and cast their crowns before the throne.

As per the 'similitude' aspect, the twenty-four orders of the Levitical priesthood officiate the morning and evening sacrifices, thus accomplishing the reconciling of committed sin. Repeating: Beyond the likelihood of them being individuals, they represented the twenty-four orders of the Levitical priesthood; the dispensation of 'Law.' The elders reflected the Law, whose effigies for sin facilitate the forgiveness of 'committed sin.' Jesus was the fulfillment of the Law; so being, from the time of his anointing in Jordan, he did then, and does now, forgive committed sin. Jesus made that fact obvious on one occasion. *"But that ye may know that the Son of man hath power on earth to forgive sins, (he saith to the sick of palsy,) I say unto thee, Arise, and take up thy bed, and go thy way unto thine house"* (Mark 2:10–11). Jesus fulfilled the Law so he embodied the Law. That is why it was said *"and in the midst of the week he shall cause the sacrifice* (daily sacrifice) *and oblation to cease"* (Daniel 9:27). Repeating: Beginning with Jesus' baptism in Jordan, the Law and the efficacy of animal sacrifice did *"cease."*

THE FOUR BEASTS (LIVING CREATURES)

VERSES 5–6. 5. *"And out of the throne proceeded lightnings and thunderings and voices: and there were seven lamps of fire burning before the throne, which are the seven Spirits of God. 6. And before the throne there was a sea of glass like unto crystal" and in the midst of the throne, and round about the throne, were four beasts full of eyes before and behind."*

This is heaven's statement and setting of the atonement, the prophesied Lamb, and that is Jesus. The text indicates the four beasts were more central to the throne of God than the twenty-four elders. Paul's thoughtful statement; *"How shall not the ministration of the spirit be rather glorious: For if the ministration of condemnation be glory, much more doth the ministration of righteousness exceed in glory"* (II Corinthians 3:8–9).

SYMBOLISMS GIVEN TO THE FOUR BEASTS

VERSES 7–8. 7. *"The first beast was like a lion, and the second beast like a calf, and the third beast had a face as a man, and the fourth beast was like a flying eagle. 8. And the four beasts had each of them six wings about him; and they were full of eyes within: and they rest not day and night, saying, Holy, holy, holy, Lord God Almighty, which was, and is, and is to come."*

The mention of the four beasts was prefaced by a reference to proceeding forth of *"lightnings and thunderings and voices."* Third heaven declarations. Furthermore, the beasts had six wings and they were full of eyes. They had covering, mobility, and promises. Matthew shows Christ fulfilling prophecy; the lion of the tribe of Judah. In Mark, he was servant-like, sacrificial. The writings of Luke portray him as man. In John, his divinity is evident. On that point; the "flying eagle" is exceptional.

The four living creatures reflect Christ's divinity. In his humanity, *"made of the seed of David according to the flesh,"* Jesus offered himself on the cross. So being: He was faithful to fulfill all prophecy as was faithful Abraham. He was sacrificial and he was human. He was the root and offspring of David. That individuality,

Jesus of Nazareth, was God's manifested *"intent."* In his body, the house God provided, he glorified his Father. And, he would himself be glorified according to God's *"Word."* Jesus prayed, *"These words spake Jesus, and lifted up his eyes to heaven, and said, Father, the hour is come; glorify thy Son, that thy Son also may glorify thee . . . And now, O Father, glorify thou me with thine own self with the glory which I had with thee before the world was"* (John 17:1, 5).

Before stated: The twenty-four elders addressed the Law and 'committed sin.' The four living creatures reflect Christ and the forgiveness of 'original sin.' Meaning this: As created, Adam was possessed by his creator. That blessed estate was lost when his flesh took leadership and the Spirit-spirit leadership became a disconnect. *"Know ye not, that to whom ye yield yourselves servants to obey, his servants ye are to whom ye obey; whether of sin unto death, or of obedience unto righteousness"* (Romans 6:16)? Adam gave himself up to sin and death. Jesus paid the price of the reconnection. Now, we, are a new man in Christ. Jesus is our atonement; term it; at-one-ment. *"For ye are bought with a price: therefore glorify God in your body, and in your spirit, which are God's . . . Ye are bought with a price; be not ye the servants of men"* (I Corinthians 6:19, 7:23). To be an overcomer is to be totally possessed of God. As per Jesus' statement: *"For the prince of this world cometh, and hath nothing in me"* (John 14:30).

GLORY AND HONOR TO GOD

VERSES 9–11. 9. *"And when those beasts give glory and honor and thanks to him that sat on the throne, who liveth for ever and ever, 10. The four and twenty elders fall down before him that sat on the throne, and worship him that liveth for ever and ever, and cast their crowns before the throne, saying, 11. Thou art worthy, O Lord, to receive glory and honor and power: for thou hast created all things, and for thy pleasure they are and were created."*

These concluding verses, including verse 8, show the four living creatures and the twenty-four elders worshipping God, without reserve, day and night. That statement equates to 'resident' worship and not a matter of 'quantity.' Like Jesus' statement to Peter to forgive seventy times seven; more a matter of 'quality' than 'quantity.' The quality manifest, like Jesus, as a 'resident' forgiving spirit. Touching overcoming and perfection: 'Resident' fruits of the spirit are the earmarks of perfection. All to the glory of God. And, *"for thy pleasure."* Truly, *"His mercy endureth forever."*

CHAPTER 5: *1. "And I saw in the right hand of him that sat on the throne a book written within and on the backside, sealed with seven seals. 2. And I saw a strong angel proclaiming with a loud voice, Who is worthy to open the book, and to loose the seals thereof? 3. And no man in heaven, nor in earth, neither under the earth, was able to open the book, neither to look thereon. 4. And I wept much, because no man was found worthy to open and to read the book, neither to look thereon. 5. And one of the elders saith unto me, Weep not: behold, the Lion of the tribe of Judah, the Root of David, hath prevailed to open the book, and to loose the seven seals thereof. 6. And I beheld, and, lo, in the midst of the throne and of the four beasts, and in the midst of the elders, stood a Lamb as it had been slain, having seven horns and seven eyes, which are the seven Spirits of God sent forth into all the earth. 7. And he came and took the book out of the right hand of him that sat upon the throne. 8. And when he had taken the book, the four beasts and four and twenty elders fell down before the Lamb, having every one of them harps, and golden vials full of odours, which are the prayers of saints. 9. And they sung a new song, saying, Thou art worthy to take the book, and to open the seals thereof: for thou wast slain, and hast redeemed us to God by thy blood out of every kindred, and tongue, and people, and nation; 10. And hast made us unto our God kings and priests: and we shall reign on the earth. 11. And I beheld, and I heard the voice of many angels round about the throne and the beasts and the elders: and the number of them was ten thousand times ten thousand, and thousands of thousands; 12. Saying with a loud voice, Worthy is the Lamb that was slain to receive power, and riches, and wisdom, and strength, and honor, and glory, and blessing. 13. And every creature which is in heaven, and on the earth, and under the earth, and such as are in the sea, and all that are in them, heard I saying, Blessing, and honor, and glory, and power, be unto him that sitteth upon the throne, and unto the Lamb for ever and ever. 14. And the four beasts said, Amen. And the four and twenty elders fell down and worshipped him that liveth for ever and ever."*

The fifth chapter continues in the presence of God's throne.

Reviewing an earlier discussed passage in Daniel 9:24: *"Seventy weeks are determined upon thy people and upon thy holy city, (1) to finish the transgression, and (2) to make an end of sins, and (3) to make reconciliation for iniquity, and (4) to bring in everlasting righteousness, and (5) to seal up the vision and prophecy, and (6) to anoint the most Holy"* (Daniel 9:24). These six mentions were concluded, or *"determined,"* on the cross when Jesus said, *"It is finished"* (John 19:30). A would-be seventh item was not mentioned. To wit: *"The times of restitution of all things, which God hath spoken by the mouth of all his holy prophets since the world began"* (Acts 3:21). That part was not in the purview of Daniel's prophesying. That part was sealed and awaited our time; the dispensing of the Revelation in John's time, and awaiting the time of happening. The above fifth mention was *"seal up the vision and prophecy."* That was determined on the cross. The unveiling was held in reserve for a future concluding time and season. Five hundred fifty years after Daniel's prophecy, John the revelator was given the Revelation of Christ. Now, nearly two centuries later, mankind is on the cutting-edge of experientially 'knowing.'

VERSES 1–5: *1. "And I saw in the right hand of him that sat on the throne a book written within and on the backside, sealed with seven seals. 2. And I saw a strong angel proclaiming with a loud voice, Who is worthy to open the book, and to loose the seals thereof? 3. And no man in heaven, nor in earth, neither under the earth, was able to open the book, neither to look thereon. 4. And I wept much, because no man was found worthy to open and to read the book, neither to look thereon. 5. And one of the elders saith unto me, Weep not: behold, the Lion of the tribe of Judah, the Root of David, hath prevailed to open the book, and to loose the seven seals thereof."*

The opening of the 'seals' are declarations, in the highest realm, toward the overturning of sin and death; the destruction of the flesh, the devil, and the world. That will accomplish the end of first heaven and first earth. This is God's *"intent,"* and glory. John *"wept much"* because the glory of God's *"intent"* was not in his preview.

The opening of the book and loosing of the seals are predicated on the basis of God imputing to Jesus the authority to reveal end-time judgments. From thence would come the happening of *"the restitution of all things."* Jesus paid the price, 'sacrifice,' and *"finished"* all that God intended.

VERSE 6: *"And I beheld, and, lo, in the midst of the throne and of the four beasts, and in the midst of the elders, stood a Lamb as it had been slain, having seven horns and seven eyes, which are the seven Spirits of God sent forth into all the earth."*

The above statement shows the disposition of the heaven-ordained setting forth of the hope of our calling; the atonement and ordination allowing the 'intermediaries' to go forth and be God's voice on earth. The similitude is the sevenfold light of the candlestick in the Holy Place.

VERSES 7–10: *7. "And he came and took the book out of the right hand of him that sat upon the throne. 8. And when he had taken the book, the four beasts and four and twenty elders fell down before the Lamb, having every one of them harps, and golden vials full of odours, which are the prayers of saints. 9. And they sung a new song, saying, Thou art worthy to take the book, and to open the seals thereof: for thou wast slain, and hast redeemed us to God by thy blood out of every kindred, and tongue, and people, and nation; 10. And hast made us unto our God kings and priests: and we shall reign on the earth."*

These verses speak of the magnitude and glory of the event of this 'Order of God' proceeding from *"Jerusalem which is above is free, which is the mother of us all"* (Galatians 4:26), and thence, unto mankind. Refreshing the principal and mandate: The message of God's plan and intent unto mankind is irrefutable. Christ is, and always was, the *"Word"*: Jesus of Nazareth, revealed in flesh as the personification of God. Faith-believing pleases God.

The *"temple,"* later *"tabernacle,"* is the place or estate that depicts God's *"Word"* as it presently abides with God in the Spirit realm. As Paul said *"which is above."* Jesus is the fullness of that *"Word"* and he, personifying God, does now dwell with God and has right to reveal God to mankind. It may be difficult to understand, but the fullness of the revelation of God's plan to mankind, through the Church officiation, has been held in reserve. It will be dispensed, in God's time, from heaven. That is the heartbeat of this discourse of 'Revelation.' Finally, literally, this revelation of God and his dear Son will tabernacle with mankind. That is, in the new heaven and the new earth. To wit: *"And I heard a great voice out of heaven saying, Behold, the tabernacle of God is with men, and he will dwell with them, and they shall be his people, and God himself shall be with them, and be their God . . . And I saw no temple therein: for the Lord God Almighty and the Lamb are the temple of it"* (Revelation 21:3, 22).

VERSES 11–14: *11. "And I beheld, and I heard the voice of many angels round about the throne and the beasts and the elders: and the number of them was ten thousand times ten thousand, and thousands of thousands; 12. Saying with a loud voice, Worthy is the Lamb that was slain to receive power, and riches, and wisdom, and strength, and honour, and glory, and blessing." 13. "And every creature which is in heaven, and on the earth, and under the earth, and such as are in the sea, and all that are in them, heard I saying, Blessing, and honour, and glory, and power, be unto him that sitteth upon the throne, and unto the Lamb for ever and ever. 14. And the four beasts said, Amen. And the four and twenty elders fell down and worshipped him that liveth for ever and ever."*

These verses refresh the opening statements of Revelation chapter 1, with the detail of the setting, in the highest heavenly realm. Also, the four living creatures are further described with the twenty-four elders worshipping and singing the praises of God and the Lamb.

The greater panorama is now included, going beyond the immediacy of the inner sanctum of God's throne. The setting remains Spirit realm, but the number is hundreds of millions. The host, in total, gives glory and honor to the Lamb. Glory and honor are declared in totality, according to the good pleasure of God and in the light of his forgiveness and restoration. Again, his mercy endures forever.

The mandate has gone forth from the highest. And, that being *"immutable,"* the text going forward, will include the voice of the intermediary officiation. The voicing of Heaven's Orders is the 'mandate,' and for the ordained officiation, it is a must-do.

Note: On that point, see Ezekiel 33:1–7: *"Again the word of the LORD came unto me, saying, Son of man, speak to the children of thy people, and say unto them, When I bring the sword upon a land, if the people of the land take a man of their coasts, and set him for their watchman: If when he seeth the sword come upon the land, he blow the trumpet, and warn the people; Then whosoever heareth the sound of the trumpet, and taketh not warning; if the sword come, and take him away, his blood shall be upon his own head. He heard the sound of the trumpet, and took not warning; his blood shall be upon him. But he that taketh warning shall deliver his soul. But if the watchman see the sword come, and blow not the trumpet, and the people be not warned; if the sword come, and take any person from among them, he is taken away in his iniquity; but his blood will I require at the watchman's hand. So thou, O son of man, I have set thee a watchman unto the house of Israel; therefore thou shalt hear the word at my mouth, and warn them from me."*

Jesus' warning and call to repentance were mostly rejected, as were the prophets of the Old Testament. And, as was Ezekiel: *"Also, thou son of man, the children of thy people still are talking against thee by the walls and in the doors of the houses, and speak one to another, every one to his brother, saying, Come, I pray you, and hear what is the word that cometh forth from the LORD. And they come unto thee as the people cometh, and they sit before thee as my people, and they hear thy words, but they will not do them: for with their mouth they shew much love, but their heart goeth after their covetousness. And, lo, thou art unto them as a very lovely song of one that hath a pleasant voice, and can play well on an instrument: for they hear thy words, but they do them not. And when this cometh to pass, (lo, it will come,) then shall they know that a prophet hath been among them"* (Ezekiel 33:30–33).

Knowing the prospect of rejection and persecution, we remember the words of Jesus: *"Enter ye in at the strait gate: for wide is the gate, and broad is the way, that leadeth to destruction, and many there be which go in thereat: Because strait is the gate, and narrow is the way, which leadeth unto life, and few there be that find it"* (Matthew 7:13–14).

CHAPTER VII

REVELATION, CHAPTER 6

CHAPTER 6: *1. "And I saw when the Lamb opened one of the seals, and I heard, as it were the noise of thunder, one of the four beasts saying, Come and see. 2. And I saw, and behold a white horse: and he that sat on him had a bow; and a crown was given unto him: and he went forth conquering, and to conquer. 3. And when he had opened the second seal, I heard the second beast say, Come and see. 4. And there went out another horse that was red: and power was given to him that sat thereon to take peace from the earth, and that they should kill one another: and there was given unto him a great sword. 5. And when he had opened the third seal, I heard the third beast say, Come and see. And I beheld, and lo a black horse; and he that sat on him had a pair of balances in his hand. 6. And I heard a voice in the midst of the four beasts say, A measure of wheat for a penny, and three measures of barley for a penny; and see thou hurt not the oil and the wine. 7. And when he had opened the fourth seal, I heard the voice of the fourth beast say, Come and see. 8. And I looked, and behold a pale horse: and his name that sat on him was Death, and Hell followed with him. And power was given unto them over the fourth part of the earth, to kill with sword, and with hunger, and with death, and with the beasts of the earth. 9. And when he had opened the fifth seal, I saw under the altar the souls of them that were slain for the word of God, and for the testimony which they held: 10. And they cried with a loud voice, saying, How long, O Lord, holy and true, dost thou not judge and avenge our blood on them that dwell on the earth? 11. And white robes were given unto every one of them; and it was said unto them, that they should rest yet for a little season, until their fellow servants also and their brethren, that should be killed as they were, should be fulfilled. 12. And I beheld when he had opened the sixth seal, and, lo, there was a great earthquake; and the sun became black as sackcloth of hair, and the moon became as blood; 13. And the stars of heaven fell unto the earth, even as a fig tree casteth her untimely figs, when she is shaken of a mighty wind. 14. And the heaven departed as a scroll when it is rolled together; and every mountain and island were moved out of their places. 15. And the kings of the earth, and the great men, and the rich men, and the chief captains, and the mighty men, and every bondman, and every free man, hid themselves in the dens and in the rocks of the mountains; 16. And said to the mountains and rocks, Fall on us, and hide us from the face of him that sitteth on the throne, and from the wrath of the Lamb: 17. For the great day of his wrath is come; and who shall be able to stand?"*

This chapter gives heaven's declaration of six seals. The first four seals occupy three and one-half years. The fifth and sixth seals occupy a second three and one-half years.

The first four seals are the season of saving grace. The Church administers salvation. Coincidentally, there are one-third judgments toward cleansing and restoration. Seals five and six reveal the closing of the Church's' mediation and the cessation of the message of salvation. Thus begins the time of martyrdom with the sealing of the saints. This writing treats the sixth seal, timewise, occurring within the last months of the three-and-one-half year time frame of the fifth seal. (Chapter 11 will give more details of the timeline of this sixth chapter, including an optional time placement of the events of the sixth seal.)

VERSES 1–8: *1. "And I saw when the Lamb opened one of the seals, and I heard, as it were the noise of thunder, one of the four beasts saying, Come and see. 2. And I saw, and behold a white horse: and he that sat on him had a bow; and a crown was given unto him: and he went forth conquering, and to conquer. 3. And when he had opened the second seal, I heard the second beast say, Come and see. 4. And there went out another horse that was red: and power was given to him that sat thereon to take peace from the earth, and that they should kill one another: and there was given unto him a great sword. 5. And when he had opened the third seal, I heard the third beast say, Come and see. And I beheld, and lo a black horse; and he that sat on him had a pair of balances in his hand. 6. And I heard a voice in the midst of the four beasts say, A measure of wheat for a penny, and three measures of barley for a penny; and see thou hurt not the oil and the wine. 7. And when he had opened the fourth seal, I heard the voice of the fourth beast say, Come and see. 8. And I looked, and behold a pale horse: and his name that sat on him was Death, and Hell followed with him. And power was given unto them over the fourth part of the earth, to kill with sword, and with hunger, and with death, and with the beasts of the earth."*

The Latter Rain church administration begins. It is the three-and-one-half year end-time message to the Gentile world. The lamb opens the seals. The declarations are as thunder from the highest realm. Jesus is the rider of the white horse. He has right to open the seals and he has the right of judgment. He has in his power the promises of God. He issues forth war, the red horse, then famine, the black horse; also, pestilence and death, the pale horse. The beasts, living creatures, referred to are those of chapter 4, verse 7: *"And the first beast was like a lion, and the second beast like a calf, and the third beast had a face as a man, and the fourth beast was like a flying eagle."* Pertaining to judgment and the mitigation of sin, Christ is all four of the living creatures. Jesus Christ is divinity. The flying eagle, unlike the landbound creatures, portrays his divinity. He conquers and purges evil, so that the promises, bow, can be given forth.

Verses 3 and 4 reveal the second seal, red horse. The face of a man. Fallen man is of the clay, as Esau, and he is red. The curse of enmity is man's lot. Enmity is separation, despising, and disdain; war and red bloodshed. Man separated from his creator, and then, carrying forward, dissensions and separations among mankind. On the solution side, Jesus, being one of mankind, was sent to heal the curse of enmity. He is the atonement, at-one-ment. Jesus is the calf. He was the lamb slain from the foundation of the earth. Here, Christ has the implements of war toward the purging of this fallen world. He is the Lion of the tribe of Judah. He has power with God toward the rulership of mankind in the restored new heaven and new earth. Verses 5 and 6 reveal the third horse, being black and depicting the curse of famine. Famine is the result of the land not yielding its fruit. Verses 7 and 8 reveal the fourth horse. The pale horse named Death and Hell.

Adam lost dominion over the creation, both plant life and animal life; macro and micro. Thus, the loss of food production, the proliferation of wild animals, pestilence, and death. Because of enmity, goes forth these; war, famine, pestilence, death, and hell. And, Hell is the estate of mankind as fallen from grace; enmity.

VERSES 9–11: *9. "And when he had opened the fifth seal, I saw under the altar the souls of them that were slain for the word of God, and for the testimony which they held: 10. And they cried with a loud voice, saying,*

How long, O Lord, holy and true, dost thou not judge and avenge our blood on them that dwell on the earth? 11. And white robes were given unto every one of them; and it was said unto them, that they should rest yet for a little season, until their fellow servants also and their brethren, that should be killed as they were, should be fulfilled."

The opening of the fifth seal begins a period of martyrdom. It is the first 'woe.' That observation is on the basis of the later statement, *"Woe, woe, woe to the inhabiters of the earth by reason of the other voices of the trumpet of the three angels, which are yet to sound."* (Revelation 8:13). The *"three angels,"* trumpet the fifth seal/first woe, sixth seal/second woe, and seventh seal/third woe. The fifth seal, first woe: The already-perfected souls *"cried with a loud voice . . . and it was said unto them, that they should rest yet for a little season . . ."* The *"little season"* is three and one-half years. It is the second three-and-one-half year season that completes a week of years. Again, the fifth seal is the first of three 'woes.' It is a season of the martyrdom of the saints.

VERSES 12–17: *12. "And I beheld when he had opened the sixth seal, and, lo, there was a great earthquake; and the sun became black as sackcloth of hair, and the moon became as blood; 13. And the stars of heaven fell unto the earth, even as a fig tree casteth her untimely figs, when she is shaken of a mighty wind. 14. And the heaven departed as a scroll when it is rolled together; and every mountain and island were moved out of their places. 15. And the kings of the earth, and the great men, and the rich men, and the chief captains, and the mighty men, and every bondman, and every free man, hid themselves in the dens and in the rocks of the mountains; 16. And said to the mountains and rocks, Fall on us, and hide us from the face of him that sitteth on the throne, and from the wrath of the Lamb: 17. For the great day of his wrath is come; and who shall be able to stand?"*

The sixth seal opening is the second 'woe.' Likely, there will be a literal earthquake. Figuratively, it refers to a world war, denoting the end of the Gentile world. It is the end-marker of Gentile times. Events are not given a time duration. Again, the sixth seal/second woe occurs in the ending months of the season of the fifth seal. Repeating: The sixth seal is not treated as a time factor on a timeline.

(As per the later accounting in chapter 11, a second event of the sixth seal/second woe is given; the Rapture: *"And they heard a great voice from heaven saying unto them, Come up hither. And they ascended up to heaven in a cloud; and their enemies beheld them. And the same hour was there a great earthquake, and the tenth part of the city fell, and in the earthquake were slain of men seven thousand: and the remnant were affrighted, and gave glory to the God of heaven. The second woe is past; and, behold, the third woe cometh quickly"* (Revelation 11:12–14). Of the two 'events,' the one talked about in this sixth chapter is the *"earthquake,"* which is likely an earthquake and a world war. Repeating: A second event is the Rapture and chapter 6 does not talk about that event.)

The ending statement, *". . . The great day of his wrath is come; and who shall be able to stand?"* introduces the seventh seal/third woe. That time will be further briefly introduced after chapter 7 at verse 1 of chapter 8. The events of the sixth seal/second woe mark the ending of Gentile times and the beginning of the Lord's Day. Events happen in rapid order. To wit: *"The second woe is past; and, behold, the third woe cometh quickly."*

CHAPTER VIII

REVELATION, CHAPTER 7

CHAPTER 7: *1. "And after these things I saw four angels standing on the four corners of the earth, holding the four winds of the earth, that the wind should not blow on the earth, nor on the sea, nor on any tree. 2. And I saw another angel ascending from the east, having the seal of the living God: and he cried with a loud voice to the four angels, to whom it was given to hurt the earth and the sea, 3. Saying, Hurt not the earth, neither the sea, nor the trees, till we have sealed the servants of our God in their foreheads. 4. And I heard the number of them which were sealed: and there were sealed an hundred and forty and four thousand of all the tribes of the children of Israel. 5. Of the tribe of Judah were sealed twelve thousand. Of the tribe of Reuben were sealed twelve thousand. Of the tribe of Gad were sealed twelve thousand. 6. Of the tribe of Aser were sealed twelve thousand. Of the tribe of Nepthalim were sealed twelve thousand. Of the tribe of Manasses were sealed twelve thousand. 7. Of the tribe of Simeon were sealed twelve thousand. Of the tribe of Levi were sealed twelve thousand. Of the tribe of Issachar were sealed twelve thousand. 8. Of the tribe of Zabulon were sealed twelve thousand. Of the tribe of Joseph were sealed twelve thousand. Of the tribe of Benjamin were sealed twelve thousand. 9. After this I beheld, and, lo, a great multitude, which no man could number, of all nations, and kindreds, and people, and tongues, stood before the throne, and before the Lamb, clothed with white robes, and palms in their hands; 10. And cried with a loud voice, saying, Salvation to our God which sitteth upon the throne, and unto the Lamb. 11. And all the angels stood round about the throne, and about the elders and the four beasts, and fell before the throne on their faces, and worshipped God, 12. Saying, Amen: Blessing, and glory, and wisdom, and thanksgiving, and honour, and power, and might, be unto our God for ever and ever. Amen. 13. And one of the elders answered, saying unto me, What are these which are arrayed in white robes? and whence came they? 14. And I said unto him, Sir, thou knowest. And he said to me, These are they which came out of great tribulation, and have washed their robes, and made them white in the blood of the Lamb. 15. Therefore are they before the throne of God, and serve him day and night in his temple: and he that sitteth on the throne shall dwell among them. 16. They shall hunger no more, neither thirst any more; neither shall the sun light on them, nor any heat. 17. For the Lamb which is in the midst of the throne shall feed them, and shall lead them unto living fountains of waters: and God shall wipe away all tears from their eyes."*

This chapter addresses the second three and one-half years period pertaining to the 'product' of 144,000 Jews and the 144,000 elect of the first resurrection.

Chapter 7 is perfectly placed. Again, it reveals the 'products' of the first five seals; both the 'terrestrial' Jew's leadership-elect and the 'celestial' first resurrection bride-elect.

VERSES 1–3: *1. "And after these things I saw four angels standing on the four corners of the earth, holding the four winds of the earth, that the wind should not blow on the earth, nor on the sea, nor on any tree. 2. And I saw another angel ascending from the east, having the seal of the living God: and he cried with a loud voice to the four angels, to whom it was given to hurt the earth and the sea, 3. Saying, Hurt not the earth, neither the sea, nor the trees, till we have sealed the servants of our God in their foreheads."*

The statement, *"Hurt not . . ."* orders the cessation of the one-third hurt put on the earth. That is a 'stop' lest further escalation wipe out the needed part that should remain. In Matthew 24:22, Jesus states, *"And except those days should be shortened, there should no flesh be saved: but for the elect's sake those days shall be shortened."* Duality of prophetic Scripture is applied here. Matthew's statement applied more exactly to the destruction of AD 67–70. Categorically, the 'end days' are addressed. This three year *"Hurt not"* pause of nature-related disasters is a preface to the pending thousand-year day of the Lord.

VERSES 4–8: *4. "And I heard the number of them which were sealed: and there were sealed an hundred and forty and four thousand of all the tribes of the children of Israel. 5. Of the tribe of Judah were sealed twelve thousand. Of the tribe of Reuben were sealed twelve thousand. Of the tribe of Gad were sealed twelve thousand. 6. Of the tribe of Aser were sealed twelve thousand. Of the tribe of Nepthalim were sealed twelve thousand. Of the tribe of Manasses were sealed twelve thousand. 7. Of the tribe of Simeon were sealed twelve thousand. Of the tribe of Levi were sealed twelve thousand. Of the tribe of Issachar were sealed twelve thousand. 8. Of the tribe of Zabulon were sealed twelve thousand. Of the tribe of Joseph were sealed twelve thousand. Of the tribe of Benjamin were sealed twelve thousand."*

These verses address the 'product' of 144,000 terrestrial Jews. As stated in verse 3, they are sealed, in Christ, for the purpose of a continuing 'terrestrial' millennium administration. The sealing is 'finished,' concluded, during the same period of persecution and martyrdom experienced by the church.

VERSES 9–17: *9. "After this I beheld, and, lo, a great multitude, which no man could number, of all nations, and kindreds, and people, and tongues, stood before the throne, and before the Lamb, clothed with white robes, and palms in their hands; 10. And cried with a loud voice, saying, Salvation to our God which sitteth upon the throne, and unto the Lamb. 11. And all the angels stood round about the throne, and about the elders and the four beasts, and fell before the throne on their faces, and worshipped God, 12. Saying, Amen: Blessing, and glory, and wisdom, and thanksgiving, and honour, and power, and might, be unto our God for ever and ever. Amen. 13. And one of the elders answered, saying unto me, What are these which are arrayed in white robes? and whence came they? 14. And I said unto him, Sir, thou knowest. And he said to me, These are they which came out of great tribulation, and have washed their robes, and made them white in the blood of the Lamb. 15. Therefore are they before the throne of God, and serve him day and night in his temple: and he that sitteth on the throne shall dwell among them. 16. They shall hunger no more, neither thirst any more; neither shall the sun light on them, nor any heat. 17. For the Lamb which is in the midst of the throne shall feed them, and shall lead them unto living fountains of waters: and God shall wipe away all tears from their eyes."*

Concurrently, timewise, verses 9 through 17 is the 'product' of the completed 144,000 man-child/bride-elect. Those are called to the throne of God and occupy a 'celestial' estate; ruling and reigning with Christ for a thousand years. Speaking of that product: *"And she brought forth a man child, who was to rule all nations with a rod of iron: and her child was caught up unto God, and to his throne"* (Revelation 12:5).

Further explanation relating to the 'concurrent' aspect of this seventh chapter: Isaiah 21:12 states, *"The watchman said, The morning cometh, and also the night: if ye will enquire, enquire ye: return, come."* Pertaining to the Jews, it is the declaring that God's promises to the Jew are going forward. The promises to Abraham and his descendants are geography-based. That is, that part pertaining to *". . . the sand of the sea, which cannot be numbered for multitude"* (Genesis 32:12). The sun will arise for them. They are going to be married to the land. It is signed, sealed, and settled, in the time of the first five seals, concluding with the 'event' of the sixth seal. That 'event' is a world war marking the end of Gentile times.

For the sake of clarity: Going forward seven and one-half years from the end of the second woe, there is again a concluding event: the Armageddon war. This war is not to be confused with the world war event of the earlier sixth seal/second woe. This war is seven and one-half years into the millennium. It is comparable to King David taking Jerusalem seven and one-half years into his reign.

Continuing Isaiah's statement: The Gentile worlds are also judged and concluded; thus, the sun goes down on the Gentile world. To wit: Isaiah 21:12 also states, *"And also the night."* So being, the Lord has gained 'product.' The remnant of the very elect is *"caught up to God, and to his throne."* That is, *"ascended up to heaven in a cloud"* (Revelation 12:5; 11:12).

Note: The language, or wording, of the ninth verse does address the celestial part. To wit: *"A great multitude, which no man could number"* is saying that it was a multitude of purpose and no man had right or privilege to qualify or quantify that host. It was 'God's Host.' As fearing God, we do confess that no man has the right to 'number' the man child, bride-elect.

CHAPTER IX

REVELATION, CHAPTERS 8-9

CHAPTER 8: *1. "And when he had opened the seventh seal, there was silence in heaven about the space of half an hour. 2. And I saw the seven angels which stood before God; and to them were given seven trumpets. 3. And another angel came and stood at the altar, having a golden censer; and there was given unto him much incense, that he should offer it with the prayers of all saints upon the golden altar which was before the throne. 4. And the smoke of the incense, which came with the prayers of the saints, ascended up before God out of the angel's hand. 5. And the angel took the censer, and filled it with fire of the altar, and cast it into the earth: and there were voices, and thunderings, and lightnings, and an earthquake. 6. And the seven angels which had the seven trumpets prepared themselves to sound. 7. The first angel sounded, and there followed hail and fire mingled with blood, and they were cast upon the earth: and the third part of trees was burnt up, and all green grass was burnt up. 8. And the second angel sounded, and as it were a great mountain burning with fire was cast into the sea: and the third part of the sea became blood; 9. And the third part of the creatures which were in the sea, and had life, died; and the third part of the ships were destroyed. 10. And the third angel sounded, and there fell a great star from heaven, burning as it were a lamp, and it fell upon the third part of the rivers, and upon the fountains of waters; 11. And the name of the star is called Wormwood: and the third part of the waters became wormwood; and many men died of the waters, because they were made bitter. 12. And the fourth angel sounded, and the third part of the sun was smitten, and the third part of the moon, and the third part of the stars; so as the third part of them was darkened, and the day shone not for a third part of it, and the night likewise. 13. And I beheld, and heard an angel flying through the midst of heaven, saying with a loud voice, Woe, woe, woe, to the inhabiters of the earth by reason of the other voices of the trumpet of the three angels, which are yet to sound!"*

Chapter 8 resumes where chapter 6 stopped. It begins with a one-verse statement addressing the seventh seal. Verse 1 is brief, but it gives heaven's status and the time duration of the seventh seal. Verse 2, chapter 8, steps back and begins addressing the first four of the seven angels opening the first four seals.

Refreshing the point: Chapter 7 was a sort of 'overview' insert addressing the 'product' of the time of the first six seals. It was informational but not a time duration factor. So being, Revelation 6:17 connects with Revelation 8:1. To wit: *6:17: "For the great day of his wrath is come; and who shall be able to stand . . . 8:1. And when he had opened the seventh seal, there was silence in heaven about the space of half an hour."* Showing this: The timeline moves from the sixth seal, which ended the second three-and-one-half year season, to the seventh seal/third woe.

VERSE 1: *1. "And when he had opened the seventh seal, there was silence in heaven about the space of half an hour."*

Verse 1 announces the opening of the seventh seal which will occupy seven and one-half years. This single verse does not reveal details of the seventh seal/third woe; only the mention. It will be detailed later. Again, the seventh seal/third woe occupies seven and one-half years. It is sevenfold; seven thunders announcing seven vials. As explained earlier, Chapter II, "Similitudes," the seventh includes seven. Again, the time duration of the third woe is *"about the space of half an hour,"* seven and one-half years. It is the "Hebron" mentioned earlier in Chapter II, "Similitudes," and, includes the "Detail Regarding David's Reign," which is the basis of the applied "Hebron" similitude.

VERSES 2–6: *2. "And I saw the seven angels which stood before God; and to them were given seven trumpets. 3. And another angel came and stood at the altar, having a golden censer; and there was given unto him much incense, that he should offer it with the prayers of all saints upon the golden altar which was before the throne. 4. And the smoke of the incense, which came with the prayers of the saints, ascended up before God out of the angel's hand. 5. And the angel took the censer, and filled it with fire of the altar, and cast it into the earth: and there were voices, and thunderings, and lightnings, and an earthquake. 6. And the seven angels which had the seven trumpets prepared themselves to sound."*

Verse 2 begins the aforementioned back-reporting of the first four seals. The time of the four living creatures and first four angels. Now begins reporting the judgment aspect of the before-portrayed first four seals in chapter 6. The time frame is three and one-half years. Coincidentally, it is the time of the Latter Rain church ministry.

Restating: Revelation 8:2 begins a sort of going back to the beginning of the first three- and-one-half year period and now giving forth heaven's judgment. As such, by verse 7 the 'determinations' are being reported and witnessed on earth. This sort of review of the matter helps the reader understand that the Church has angelic, heaven-backed officiation. Again, three and one-half years ministry which will conclude Gentile church operation, and that time frame corresponds with the first four seals of Revelation 6:1–8.

VERSES 7–12: *7. "The first angel sounded, and there followed hail and fire mingled with blood, and they were cast upon the earth: and the third part of trees was burnt up, and all green grass was burnt up. 8. And the second angel sounded, and as it were a great mountain burning with fire was cast into the sea: and the third part of the sea became blood; 9. And the third part of the creatures which were in the sea, and had life, died; and the third part of the ships were destroyed. 10. And the third angel sounded, and there fell a great star from heaven, burning as it were a lamp, and it fell upon the third part of the rivers, and upon the fountains of waters; 11. And the name of the star is called Wormwood: and the third part of the waters became wormwood; and many men died of the waters, because they were made bitter. 12. And the fourth angel sounded, and the third part of the sun was smitten, and the third part of the moon, and the third part of the stars; so as the third part of them was darkened, and the day shone not for a third part of it, and the night likewise."*

Revelation 8:2 gives the transitioning of heaven's statement unto the Church and thence to mankind. And thence, the first four seals revealed this transitioning of God's plan and determinations; transitioned unto man by the church officiation. It is the time of mitigated judgment; war, famine, and pestilence.

Revelation 8:7–12 shows the judgments as one-third limited. A three-and-one-half year window of opportunity; the *"come out of her"* message. The time, duration, is three and one-half years. It is the 'Latter Rain' season of Church officiation.

The seven angels give unto mankind God's declarations of judgment upon the earth. The first four angels occupy the same three-and-one-half-year time frame as the four horses of Revelation chapter 6, verses 2 through 8. The declarations, and then the mandate, is the Church's estate of 'power with God.' To wit: *"These have power to shut heaven, that it rain not in the days of their prophecy: and have power over waters to turn them to blood, and to smite the earth with all plagues, as often as they will"* (Revelation 11:6). This three-and-one-half year time of the four seals/trumpets/angels is the Latter Rain. We see God's limited judgment on all green grass, the sea, the creatures which were in the sea, the ships, the rivers and the fountains of waters, and the sun and moon and stars. These are literal signs in the earth, witnessed by all of mankind.

Refreshing the applicable Scripture: Revelation 18:4. The *"voice from heaven, saying, Come out of her my people"* has been declared. That command *"Come out"* is an abiding and ongoing call to the individual heart. With respect to the whole body of nations, God's directives will have been sounded and the mediation accomplished by the ending of the Church operation, at which time the fifth angel/first woe begins.

Restating earlier comments concerning the soon coming Church-advent: Predating the Latter Rain, the knowledge of the end-time will be more perfectly revealed. The understanding will be entrusted to ordained ministers who will convey God's will to mankind. The Latter Church operation; *"And hath raised us up together, and made us sit together in heavenly places in Christ Jesus."* And, *"For our conversation is in heaven; from whence also we look for the Saviour, the Lord Jesus Christ"* (Ephesians 2:6; Philippians 3:20). As per Paul's statement: *"How then shall they call upon him in whom they have not believed? And how shall they believe in him of whom they have not heard? And how shall they hear without a preacher? And how shall they preach, except they be sent"* (Romans 10:14, 15)? Both the reporting and compliance are a "holy place" operation.

VERSE 13: *"And I beheld, and heard an angel flying through the midst of heaven, saying with a loud voice, Woe, woe, woe, to the inhabiters of the earth by reason of the other voices of the trumpet of the three angels, which are yet to sound!"*

This declaration equates to an introduction of the approaching time of the unmitigated judgments of God. So being, they are termed "woes." That now follows: The trumpeting from heaven of the last three seals/angels; five, six, and seven.

CHAPTER 9: *1. "And the fifth angel sounded, and I saw a star fall from heaven unto the earth: and to him was given the key of the bottomless pit. 2. And he opened the bottomless pit; and there arose a smoke out of the pit, as the smoke of a great furnace; and the sun and the air were darkened by reason of the smoke of the pit. 3. And there came out of the smoke locusts upon the earth: and unto them was given power, as the scorpions of the earth have power. 4. And it was commanded them that they should not hurt the grass of the earth, neither any green thing, neither any tree; but only those men which have not the seal of God in their foreheads. 5. And to them it was given that they should not kill them, but that they should be tormented five months: and their torment was as the torment of a scorpion, when he striketh a man. 6. And in those days shall men seek death, and shall not find it; and shall desire to die, and death shall flee from them. 7. And the shapes of the locusts were like unto horses prepared unto battle; and on their heads were as it were crowns like gold, and their faces were as the faces of men. 8. And they had hair as the hair of women, and their teeth were as the teeth of lions. 9. And they had breastplates, as it were breastplates of iron; and the sound of their wings was as the sound of chariots of many horses running to battle. 10. And they had tails like unto scorpions, and there were stings in their tails: and their power was to hurt men five months. 11. And they had a king over them, which is the angel of the bottomless pit, whose name in the Hebrew tongue is Abaddon, but in the Greek tongue hath his name Apollyon. 12. One woe is past; and, behold, there come two woes more hereafter. 13. And the sixth angel sounded, and I heard a voice from the four horns of the golden altar which is before God, 14. Saying to the sixth angel which had the trumpet, Loose the four angels which are bound in the great river Euphrates. 15. And the four angels were loosed, which were prepared for an hour, and a day, and a month, and a year, for to slay the third part of men. 16. And the number of the army of the horsemen were two hundred thousand thousand: and I heard the number of them. 17. And thus I saw the horses in the vision, and them that sat on them, having breastplates of fire, and of jacinth, and brimstone: and the heads of the horses were as the heads of lions; and out of their mouths issued fire and smoke and brimstone. 18. By these three was the third part of men killed, by the fire, and by the smoke, and by the brimstone, which issued out of their mouths. 19. For their power is in their mouth, and in their tails: for their tails were like unto serpents, and had heads, and with them they do hurt. 20. And the rest of the men which were not killed by these plagues yet repented not of the works of their hands, that they should not worship devils, and idols of gold, and silver, and brass, and stone, and of wood: which neither can see, nor hear, nor walk: 21. Neither repented they of their murders, nor of their sorceries, nor of their fornication, nor of their thefts."*

Chapter 9 is a continuation of chapter 8. Now begins the woes. It is the time of the fifth seal/first woe and the events of the sixth seal/second woe. It is a second period of three and one-half years. Again, the transition is from fourth seal to fifth seal. What is vital is the change from 'mediation' to 'woes' having no mediation. (Revelation 6:9–11 revealed this same fifth seal period, but in terms of a *"little season"* of the martyrdom of the saints.)

VERSE 1: *"And the fifth angel sounded, and I saw a star fall from heaven unto the earth: and to him was given the key of the bottomless pit."*

The statement *"fall from heaven"* connects with Revelation 12:9: *"And the great dragon was cast out, that old serpent, called the Devil, and Satan, which deceiveth the whole world: he was cast out into the earth, and his angels were cast out with him."* At that time, having been given the *"key of the bottomless pit,"* the Devil had right to lose the other evil spirits who were bound. To wit, those spoken of in Jude 6, *"And the angels which kept not their first estate, but left their own habitation, he hath reserved in everlasting chains under darkness unto the judgment of the great day."* This event of *"Satan . . . he was cast out into the earth, and his angels . . ."* is the *"judgment of the great day."* The result will be many thousands who are not 'sealed' in Christ becoming possessed by evil spirits. That resulting judgment of 'possession' denotes the movement from seventh beast to the eighth beast. Revelation 17:11 refers to the end state of the eighth beast. *"And the beast that was, and is not, even he is the eight, and is of the seven, and goeth into perdition."* In context, that is the judgment of the realms of heaven and earth.

VERSES 2–6: *2. "And he opened the bottomless pit; and there arose a smoke out of the pit, as the smoke of a great furnace; and the sun and the air were darkened by reason of the smoke of the pit. 3. And there came out of the smoke locusts upon the earth: and unto them was given power, as the scorpions of the earth have power. 4. And it was commanded them that they should not hurt the grass of the earth, neither any green thing, neither any tree; but only those men which have not the seal of God in their foreheads. 5. And to them it was given that they should not kill them, but that they should be tormented five months: and their torment was as the torment of a scorpion, when he striketh a man. 6. And in those days shall men seek death, and shall not find it; and shall desire to die, and death shall flee from them."*

Transitioning to the fifth angel/fifth seal/first woe, the one-third hurt put on the earth ceases. To wit: *"Hurt not the earth, neither the sea, nor the trees, till we have sealed the servants of our God in their foreheads"* (Revelation 7:3). The 'hurting' now passes from the natural earth to living mankind. (Reminiscent of Job's temptation, as his testing graduated from his possessions to his person.) This 'first woe,' totaling three and one-half years, will include in its ending months, the *"short time"* of the eighth beast, *"And he doeth great wonders, so that he maketh fire come down from heaven on the earth in the sight of men"* (Revelation 13:13). Repeating: The time frame of the fifth seal/first woe is three and one-half years. (Chapter 9 does not report the concurrent persecution of the Church and the death of the saints which occupy this time of the fifth seal/first woe. It does report an overview of the judgment of the wicked.)

VERSES 7–11: *7. "And the shapes of the locusts were like unto horses prepared unto battle; and on their heads were as it were crowns like gold, and their faces were as the faces of men. 8. And they had hair as the hair of women, and their teeth were as the teeth of lions. 9. And they had breastplates, as it were breastplates of iron; and the sound of their wings was as the sound of chariots of many horses running to battle. 10. And they had tails like unto scorpions, and there were stings in their tails: and their power was to hurt men five months. 11. And they had a king over them, which is the angel of the bottomless pit, whose name in the Hebrew tongue is Abaddon, but in the Greek tongue hath his name Apollyon."*

These characterizations given in these verses depict the evil disposition of war. God is a Spirit. When he addresses a matter, it is a spiritual, dispositional reflection. For example, as per Revelation 6:4, the evil wrought upon mankind with the advent of the red horse rider and his blood-sword are as real as the literal event of the war itself. And so is this text a 'God-reflection' regarding the 'nature' of the contest. The fifth seal/first woe is concluding and the events of the sixth seal/second woe are eminent.

Concerning the Church: The fifth seal/first woe is the time of unmitigated spiritual opposition; Satan, moving from spirit realm into the fallen estate of material realm. That is reminiscent of Noah's time when the heavens were judged and two-thirds were cast down from the spirit realm to the material realm. Thus, eventually, as the spirits going into the swine, they were without the advantage of possessing a body. Jude 6 states, they *"kept not their first estate . . . left their own habitation . . . under darkness,"* most likely disembodied. We see that reality evidenced in the New Testament. The remaining one-third of the evil entities, having retained their spirit habitation, could and did continue to oppress, distress, suppress, and even possess living creatures.

VERSES 12–14: *12. "One woe is past; and, behold, there come two woes more hereafter. 13. And the sixth angel sounded, and I heard a voice from the four horns of the golden altar which is before God, 14. Saying to the sixth angel which had the trumpet, Loose the four angels which are bound in the great river Euphrates."*

The ending phase of the first woe goes forward quickly to the second woe which are the ending 'events' of mankind's six thousand years. The *"five months,"* verses 5 and 10, are within the time frame of three and one-half years given to the fifth seal.

Repeating the thought: The fifth seal opens a season of three and one-half years persecution and martyrdom of God's people. A five-month season, inclusive of the fifth seal, will be a time of pain and torment on the flesh of *"those men which have not the seal of God in their foreheads."* Again, it is preparatory toward a third world war. The level of conflict graduates from the flesh-and-blood realm to include spiritual warfare. The urgency of that prospect will be brought to bear when the heavens are brought to God's judgment seat as it was in the days of Noah. *"Yea, the heavens are not clean in his sight"* (Job 15:15). And, *"Know ye not that we shall judge angels?"* (I Corinthians 6:3).

The sixth angel declares the second woe which is the 'event' of a world war. Repeating the premise: Preparatory to this war is the loosing, or cessation, of the holding-back mandate as stated in Revelation 7:1–3. *1. "And after these things I saw four angels standing on the four corners of the earth, holding the four winds of the earth, that the wind should not blow on the earth, nor on the sea, nor on any tree. 7:2 And I saw another angel ascending from the east, having the seal of the living God: and he cried with a loud voice to the four angels, to whom it was given to hurt the earth and the sea, 7:3 Saying, Hurt not the earth, neither the sea, nor the trees, till we have sealed the servants of our God in their foreheads."* The holding-back mandate was given in light of the necessary pause for the sealing of the product of the first four seals/horses of the three-and-one-half year Latter Rain church operation. At this point in the text, that 'holding back' is no longer in effect. 'This point' being the transitioning of the first woe to the second woe. The products are sealed and Satan is cast into the earth.

Again, *"five months"* of verses 5 and 10 occur within the three-and-one-half-year time frame of the fifth seal. The sixth seal's 'events' of the Rapture and a world war are like the 'period' at the end of a sentence. Note: The end-time events, sixth seal, mark the end of Gentile times and the beginning of Christ' millennium reign.

VERSE 15: *"And the four angels were loosed, which were prepared for an hour, and a day, and a month, and a year, for to slay the third part of men."*

Verse 15 gives time measures. Time measures have implied meaning. *"Hour"* relates to God's judgment unto restoration. *"Day"* is sun-related and refers to the Christ and the Church operation: God's Body of Christ and second witness to his presence. *"Month"* is moon-related and refers to the Jews, God's chosen people and his timepiece on earth. *"Year"* is Christ's day and speaks to the restoring of all things. The statement *"for to slay the third part of men"* could be the giving again of their original description and function. The one-third limit will be removed after the sealing that is 'finished' at the time of the second woe. Thence, going forward in time to the time of Armageddon. The term *'time of Armageddon'* is used to denote the time *"he gathered them together into a place called in the Hebrew tongue Armageddon."* That time frame would be the seven plus years until the event of the Armageddon war. The 'gathering' would include the time of the formation of the two-hundred-million-man army that was gathering, present tense, in the face of a Third World War.

Some may remember the hope expressed post-WWI: 'The War to End All Wars.' The world could see a like disappointment. Another major war will follow the failed hope of *". . . when they say peace and safety"* (I Thessalonians 5:3). The Jews will dismiss the occupying peace forces from Jerusalem. Most have heard the term *'Samson complex.'* That mindset may be on our doorstep. If that, or some like-scenario develops, the nations of the world will act multilaterally. However good-intended, the powers of this world will lose whatever control they have. God and our Lord takes control and the third woe comes to bear. That is the time of thunders and vials being poured out and the season is seven and one-half years of 'Armageddon time.' It ends with the 'happening' of the Armageddon war. The two-hundred-million-man army will be gathering and poised and then sweep the Middle East. The army will aim to cleanse the earth of Jew and Arab, Judaism and Islam. Zechariah 13:8 indicates that only one-third of the Jews will survive. It is a 'duality' with AD 67–70. *"And except those days should be shortened, there should no flesh be saved: but for the elect's sake those days shall be shortened"* (Matthew 24:22). The Lord shows himself strong in the Armageddon war event to save the one-third remanent, being the sealed, converted Jews. That will include the Church remnant that happens to be present in that geography. *"Then shall the Lord go forth, and fight against those nations, as when he fought in the day of battle . . ."And ye shall flee to the valley of the mountains; for the valley of the mountains shall reach unto Azal: yea, ye shall flee, like as ye fled from before the earthquake in the days of Uzziah king of Judah; and the Lord my God shall come, and all the saints with thee"* (Zechariah 14:3, 5).

The mention of *"the great river Euphrates"* gives the placement of the four angels. The four are the same four, Christ-based, being God's voice, seals or declarations to mankind. Early on, they were mediation-like, but here, as-unto-judgment. The *"river Euphrates"* is many things to mankind; a boundary, a source of life sustaining water, or even an object of worship, idolatry-like. In a 'societal' sense, it could reflect the compassion and patience of the world's population and governments. Later, in the time of Armageddon, all patience is exhausted. *"The water thereof was dried up"* (Revelation 16:12).

VERSES 16–21: *16. "And the number of the army of the horsemen were two hundred thousand thousand: and I heard the number of them. 17. And thus I saw the horses in the vision, and them that sat on them, having breastplates of fire, and of jacinth, and brimstone: and the heads of the horses were as the heads of lions; and out of their mouths issued fire and smoke and brimstone. 18. By these three was the third part of men killed, by the fire, and by the smoke, and by the brimstone, which issued out of their mouths. 19. For their power is in their mouth, and in their tails: for their tails were like unto serpents, and had heads, and with them they do hurt. 20. And the rest of the men which were not killed by these plagues yet repented not of the works of their hands, that they should not worship devils, and idols of gold, and silver, and brass, and stone, and of wood: which neither can see, nor hear, nor walk: 21. Neither repented they of their murders, nor of their sorceries, nor of their fornication, nor of their thefts."*

The number of the army is two hundred million. Reasonably, that number includes the support that it takes to field the fighting troops. The Far Eastern nations, including nations to the north, could field such a war machine. Again, the above depiction is as much 'dispositional' as it is literal. God didn't' show John the detail of the instruments of war. Advanced weapons of modern warfare will be essentially exhausted in the world war that predates the 'time of Armageddon.'

There is no repentance in the time of the end when all mediation has ceased. Blindness is total. No light, however bright, is perceptible; only the 'heat' of judgment.

CHAPTER X
REVELATION, CHAPTER 10

CHAPTER 10: *1. "And I saw another mighty angel come down from heaven, clothed with a cloud: and a rainbow was upon his head, and his face was as it were the sun, and his feet as pillars of fire: 2. And he had in his hand a little book open: and he set his right foot upon the sea, and his left foot on the earth, 3. And cried with a loud voice, as when a lion roareth: and when he had cried, seven thunders uttered their voices. 4. And when the seven thunders had uttered their voices, I was about to write: and I heard a voice from heaven saying unto me, Seal up those things which the seven thunders uttered, and write them not. 5. And the angel which I saw stand upon the sea and upon the earth lifted up his hand to heaven, 6. And sware by him that liveth for ever and ever, who created heaven, and the things that therein are, and the earth, and the things that therein are, and the sea, and the things which are therein, that there should be time no longer: 7. But in the days of the voice of the seventh angel, when he shall begin to sound, the mystery of God should be finished, as he hath declared to his servants the prophets. 8. And the voice which I heard from heaven spake unto me again, and said, Go and take the little book which is open in the hand of the angel which standeth upon the sea and upon the earth. 9. And I went unto the angel, and said unto him, Give me the little book. And he said unto me, Take it, and eat it up; and it shall make thy belly bitter, but it shall be in thy mouth sweet as honey. 10. And I took the little book out of the angel's hand, and ate it up; and it was in my mouth sweet as honey: and as soon as I had eaten it, my belly was bitter. 11. And he said unto me, Thou must prophesy again before many peoples, and nations, and tongues, and kings."*

It is the declaration of the seventh angel; the time of the seventh seal/third woe. The beginning seven and one-half years of Christ's millennium reign.

VERSE 1–3: *1. "And I saw another mighty angel come down from heaven, clothed with a cloud: and a rainbow was upon his head, and his face was as it were the sun, and his feet as pillars of fire: 2. And he had in his hand a little book open: and he set his right foot upon the sea, and his left foot on the earth, 3. And cried with a loud voice, as when a lion roareth: and when he had cried, seven thunders uttered their voices."*

This *"mighty angel"* is forceful and overpowering. This is Christ reflecting omnipotence. He occupies land and sea and has the right and justification to declare God's final judgments on all the earth. Daniel's prophetic statement shows us an Old Testament comparable relating to the 'Prophesied Christ.' *"Then I Daniel looked, and, behold, there stood other two, the one on this side of the bank of the river, and the other on that side of the bank of the river. 6. And one said to the man clothed in linen, which was upon the waters of the river, how long shall it be to the end of these wonders? 7. And I heard the man clothed in linen, which was upon the waters of the river, when he held up his right hand and his left hand unto heaven, and sware by him that liveth for ever that it shall be for a time, times, and an half; and when he shall have accomplished to scatter the power of the holy people, all these things shall be finished"* (Daniel 12:5–7).

Being more explicit regarding the above quote: Daniel lived in the approximate time frame of 540 BC to 450 BC. He prophesied in the approximate time frame of 500 BC. The heart of prophecy is Jesus Christ. *"For the testimony of Jesus is the spirit of prophecy"* (Revelation 19:10). In Daniel's writing, Jesus was *"the man clothed in linen"* and the two that stood on either side of the river were likely Michael and Gabriel. *"These are the two anointed ones, that stand by the Lord of the whole earth"* (Zechariah 4:14). The point of emphasis here: Our Lord and Savior Jesus Christ is the Heart of God and is Beloved of the Father. As stated in the beginning, it is *"the Revelation of Jesus Christ."* The *"little book"* denotes a scroll or tablet; the Greek term from which we have the English word *'Bible.'* In God's omniscience, it reasonably includes God's *"Word,"* to wit: Christ, the plan of the ages, and inclusive to that is *"the book of life."*

VERSES 4–7: *4. "And when the seven thunders had uttered their voices, I was about to write: and I heard a voice from heaven saying unto me, Seal up those things which the seven thunders uttered, and write them not. 5. And the angel which I saw stand upon the sea and upon the earth lifted up his hand to heaven, 6. And sware by him that liveth for ever and ever, who created heaven, and the things that therein are, and the earth, and the things that therein are, and the sea, and the things which are therein, that there should be time no longer: 7. But in the days of the voice of the seventh angel, when he shall begin to sound, the mystery of God should be finished, as he hath declared to his servants the prophets."*

The seven thunders are the third 'woe.' Seven vials poured out without mitigation. No daysman, no intermediary, no safety of the Church. At that point, John was told, *"Write them not."* This *"seventh angel"* standing *"upon the sea and upon the earth"* has the right to both open or *"seal up those things which the seven thunders uttered."* The emphasis here is that *"there should be time no longer."* It is implicit in the text: No distraction or future speculation. The mystery will be *"finished"* at the time the seven thunders begin to sound. God wants the world to know that Gentile times, man's six thousand years, is over and done.

VERSES 8–11: *8. "And the voice which I heard from heaven spake unto me again, and said, Go and take the little book which is open in the hand of the angel which standeth upon the sea and upon the earth. 9. And I went unto the angel, and said unto him, Give me the little book. And he said unto me, Take it, and eat it up; and it shall make thy belly bitter, but it shall be in thy mouth sweet as honey. 10. And I took the little book out of the angel's hand, and ate it up; and it was in my mouth sweet as honey: and as soon as I had eaten it, my belly was bitter. 11. And he said unto me, Thou must prophesy again before many peoples, and nations, and tongues, and kings."*

At this point, the *"mighty angel"* addresses John and gives him a mandate and commission. He receives the orders, and the 'hearing' is *"sweet as honey,"* but the 'doing' is *"bitter."* The book of Revelation is a continuing "prophesy" to peoples and nations.

CHAPTER XI

REVELATION, CHAPTER 11

Revelation 11 gives us both events and timeline of God's declarations. Revelation chapter 4 begins things ordained and declared, in the Spirit realm, pertaining to God's plan of judgment. The dispensing is per his determination. The revealing of his plan and all fulfillments will be according to his 'intent.' God is Sovereign. God is Omnipotent. Man's time and season have beginnings and endings. God ordains and institutes judgment. He is subject to no schedule. He initiates his just will and concludes matters as his will determines. We see a timeline, and there is a 'beginning' to the operation of the Church in this last hour. It bears repeating: 'Events' are markers denoting endings and/or the beginnings. Among the ecclesia, in the overview, the Revelation-understanding is termed *'the end-time message.'*

CHAPTER 11: *1. "And there was given me a reed like unto a rod: and the angel stood, saying, Rise, and measure the temple of God, and the altar, and them that worship therein. 2. But the court which is without the temple leave out, and measure it not; for it is given unto the Gentiles: and the holy city shall they tread under foot forty and two months. 3. And I will give power unto my two witnesses, and they shall prophesy a thousand two hundred and threescore days, clothed in sackcloth. 4. These are the two olive trees, and the two candlesticks standing before the God of the earth. 5. And if any man will hurt them, fire proceedeth out of their mouth, and devoureth their enemies: and if any man will hurt them, he must in this manner be killed. 6. These have power to shut heaven, that it rain not in the days of their prophecy: and have power over waters to turn them to blood, and to smite the earth with all plagues, as often as they will. 7. And when they shall have finished their testimony, the beast that ascendeth out of the bottomless pit shall make war against them, and shall overcome them, and kill them. 8. And their dead bodies shall lie in the street of the great city, which spiritually is called Sodom and Egypt, where also our Lord was crucified. 9. And they of the people and kindreds and tongues and nations shall see their dead bodies three days and an half, and shall not suffer their dead bodies to be put in graves. 10. And they that dwell upon the earth shall rejoice over them, and make merry, and shall send gifts one to another; because these two prophets tormented them that dwelt on the earth. 11. And after three days and an half the Spirit of life from God entered into them, and they stood upon their feet; and great fear fell upon them which saw them. 12. And they heard a great voice from heaven saying unto them, Come up hither. And they ascended up to heaven in a cloud; and their enemies beheld them. 13. And the same hour was there a great earthquake, and the tenth part of the city fell, and in the earthquake were slain of men seven thousand: and the remnant were affrighted, and gave glory to the God of heaven. 14. The second woe is past; and, behold, the third woe cometh quickly. 15. And the seventh angel sounded; and there were great voices in heaven, saying, The kingdoms of this world are become the kingdoms of our Lord, and of his Christ; and he shall reign for ever and ever. 16. And the four and twenty elders, which sat before God on their seats, fell upon their faces, and worshipped God, 17. Saying, We give thee thanks, O Lord God Almighty, which art, and wast, and art to come; because thou hast taken to thee thy great power, and hast reigned. 18. And the nations were angry, and thy wrath is come, and the time of the dead, that they should be judged, and that thou shouldest give reward unto thy servants the prophets, and to the saints, and them that fear thy name, small and great; and shouldest destroy them which destroy the earth. 19. And the temple of God was opened in heaven, and there was seen in his temple the ark of his testament: and there were lightnings, and voices, and thunderings, and an earthquake, and great hail."*

Chapters 7, 10, and later, 14, were introduced to give the details of events with respect to the product. As such, those chapters were pauses in terms of progressing on the 'timeline' of events. Chapter 11 gives the details of events, but additionally, it provides us with the timing of events. So that, at this point in the writing, we can amplify on the duration, or season, ascribed to the events of the last hour. The mandate to *"measure,"* mentioned in the first verse, marks the beginning events of the last hour.

THE TIMELINE ASPECT

THE FIRST THREE AND ONE-HALF YEARS is the season of the first four seals revealing four horses. It is the time of both the Latter Rain church and, concurrently, the beginning of the 'sealing' of terrestrial Jews fitted for in-the-earth leadership. That Jewish terrestrial leadership will continue into the Lord's one-thousand-year day. Note: The natural seed of Abraham and the spiritual seed of Abraham, by faith, will integrate seamlessly into one unified new man in the new heaven and new earth. There will be no second-class citizens in the new heaven.

THE SECOND THREE AND ONE-HALF YEARS is the noted duration of the fifth seal/first woe. The ending months of the fifth seal time frame will include the 'events' of the great earthquake and the catching away. These events of a world war and the Rapture are the sixth seal/second woe. In total, both the fifth and sixth seals are a season of martyrdom of God's elect at the hands of man and demon. *'And demon'* because it is the season of the *"eighth beast"* (Revelation 17:11). And, the 'eighth beast' is manifest and equates to the addition of demons into the earth's judgments.

CONCERNING DEMONS AND THE JUDGMENT OF SPIRIT REALM ENTITIES: Job stated, *"Yea, the heavens are not clean in his sight."* Paul stated, *"Know ye not that we shall judge angels? How much more things that pertain to this life?"* (Job 15:15, I Corinthians 6:3). The apostle Peter makes a difference between those things fleshly and those things demonic. To wit: *"Whereas angels, which are greater in power and might, bring not railing accusations against them before the Lord"* (II Peter 2:11).

The cry goes up from the highest heaven, *"How long, O Lord, holy and true, doest thou not judge and avenge our blood on them that dwell on the earth? And white robes were given unto every one of them; and it was said unto them, that they should rest yet for a little season, until their fellow servants also and their brethren, that should be killed as they were, should be fulfilled"* (Revelation 6:10–11). This *"little season"* is this second three-and-one-half year time frame of the fifth seal/first woe, up to and including the sixth seal/second woe.

John sees Satan cast out of his heavenly estate into the realm of humanity. It is noteworthy that the same *"cast them down"* or *"fall from heaven"* happened in Noah's time. *"For if God spared not the angels that sinned, but cast them down to hell, and delivered them into chains of darkness, to be reserved unto judgment; And spared not the old world, but saved Noah the eighth person, a preacher of righteousness, bringing in the flood upon the world of the ungodly"* (II Peter 2:4–5).

Satan is both instigator and leader of rebellion against God. The eighth beast is the working of a cast-out Satan to possess men and work evil against the remanent of the Church.

"The beast that thou sawest was, and is not; and shall ascend out of the bottomless pit, and go into perdition: and they that dwell on the earth shall wonder, whose names were not written in the book of life from the foundation of the world, when they behold the beast that was, and is not, and yet is" (Revelation 17:8).

The eighth beast is an extension of the seventh. Spirit entities and flesh entities are united in their opposition to God and both realms will persecute God's elect. Again, spirit realm and flesh realm joined in opposition against God. Repeating: 'Woes' are declared because God's judgment sounds from heaven and 'mediation' has ceased. The time of the fifth seal/first woe, *". . . When they* (the mediating voice of the Lord's Church) *shall have finished their testimony . . ."* (Revelation 11:7).

CONCERNING OUR PART AS MORTALS, and pertaining to this time of martyrdom: *"Whereas angels, which are greater in power and might, bring not railing accusations against them before the Lord"* (II Peter 2:11). It is not the saints' crying out and pointing a finger of accusation. That is what Satan does. Our calling is to live and die as an example of God's love for mankind. Jesus is our perfect example. Jesus did oppose Satan and he cast out devils, but in the matter of his literal death, he died in agony on the cross. In dying, he stated, *"Forgive them."* In Christ's likeness, we are blessed by God. We are justified in Christ. Let us die daily and hope to be that martyr that dies 'the death' literally. For certainty, God judged the nation, but in the instance of the cross, Jesus stayed out of his Father's chair. Let us follow Christ's example. Concerning *"him that had the power of death, that is, the devil . . ."* Jude stated, *"The Lord rebuke thee"* (Hebrews 2:14, Jude 9).

The sixth seal/second woe is an event. It is given no time duration other than the mention of five months (9:5, 10). It is a marker of both the end of the fifth seal/first woe and the beginning of the seventh seal/third woe. Essentially, the sixth seal/second woe is the clarion declaration of 'endings and beginnings.' This sixth seal is the great earthquake, a world war, and, forthwith, the Rapture. The 'Rapture,' as per King James: *"They ascended up to heaven in a cloud; and their enemies beheld them"* (Revelation 11:12). This is the same *"caught up unto God, and to his throne"* (Revelation 12:5). It is the notable beginning of the 'Hebron' time of seven and one-half years. Again, the sixth seal/second woe is both the war concluding Gentile times, and the Rapture declaring the coming seventh seal/third woe. Going forward, *"The kingdoms of this world are become the kingdoms of our Lord, and of his Christ; and he shall reign for ever and ever"* (Revelation 11:15). This seventh seal/third woe *"cometh quickly."* It is the day of the Lord and the seventh includes seven; the wrath of God sevenfold. Seven thunders declaring seven vials poured into the earth.

VERSES 1–2: *1. "And there was given me a reed like unto a rod: and the angel stood, saying, Rise, and measure the temple of God, and the altar, and them that worship therein. 2. But the court which is without the temple leave out, and measure it not; for it is given unto the Gentiles: and the holy city shall they tread under foot forty and two months."*

The *"measure"* begins the first three and one-half years of the last hour. Gentile powers occupy Jerusalem and, in that same time frame, four seals are opened. It is the time of the Latter Rain.

"Months" are moon-reckoned and pertain to the Jew. *"Forty and two months"* is three and one-half years. *"The court which is without the temple"* refers to the physical geography. With the exception of the Temple Mount, Gentile powers will be in control of the landscape. That control will be with the Jews' reluctant agreement. The religious part, *"The temple of God, and the altar, and them that worship therein,"* will not be under Gentile rule during these three and one-half years. Even now, an incident of the magnitude sufficient to provoke a world government intervention and oversight of Jerusalem is becoming more believable. Likely, it will be initiated in the face of a ramping-up toward a world war. Necessarily, responsible world bodies will step up and make fitting judgments toward an international peacekeeping force. Tragically, God and our Lord Christ will not be a party to whatever steps are taken. That is why the whole of the matter is categorized as *"the beast."* Considering such a peacekeeping force, it would be that time when men say, *"Peace and safety"* (I Thessalonians 5:3). The Jew's time and space for tolerating such an occupation is likely three and one-half years. If one-third speaks of a judgment then two-thirds is judgment complete; purification of the Chosen Jews. Revelation 7:1–8 speaks to that 'product.' On that point, Zechariah 13:9 speaks to that 'purification.' *"And I will bring the third part through the fire, and will refine them as silver is refined, and will try them as gold is tried: they shall call on my name, and I will hear them: I will say, It is my people: and they shall say, The Lord is my God."*

From the onset, Mediterranean powers will likely take a determined position. To wit: *"And the ten horns which thou sawest are ten kings, which have received no kingdom as yet; but receive power as kings one hour with the beast. These have one mind, and shall give their power and strength unto the beast"* (Revelation 17:12–13).

VERSES 3–6: *3 "And I will give power unto my two witnesses, and they shall prophesy a thousand two hundred and threescore days, clothed in sackcloth. 4. These are the two olive trees, and the two candlesticks standing before the God of the earth. 5. And if any man will hurt them, fire proceedeth out of their mouth, and devoureth their enemies: and if any man will hurt them, he must in this manner be killed. 6. These have power to shut heaven, that it rain not in the days of their prophecy: and have power over waters to turn them to blood, and to smite the earth with all plagues, as often as they will."*

Referring to *"my two witnesses,"* the prophet states it thus: *"These are the two anointed ones, that stand by the Lord of the whole earth"* (Zechariah 4:14). In the same vein, the angel Gabriel stated: *"I am Gabriel, that stand in the presence of God"* (Luke 1:19). These *"two witnesses"* show the heavenly declaration toward God's ordained ministry on earth; which 'officiation' are called to obedience. The flesh and blood aspect of this mandate, with power, includes the giving of their natural lives.

On that point of God-ordained mediation in the earth: This three and one-half years, concluding Latter Rain operation, will be the 'Elijah ministry.' Reasonably, it is a duality of the interpretation of Malachi 4:5–6: *"Behold, I will send you Elijah the prophet before the coming of the great and dreadful day of the Lord: And he shall turn the heart of the fathers to the children, and the heart of the children to their fathers, lest I come and smite the earth with a curse."* The basis of this duality, the ministry of the Church to the Gentiles, overlays that part of the Early Rain church pertaining particularly to the three and one-half years from Pentecost till the stoning of Stephen. These Early and Latter Rain ministries are one beaten piece of gold in the Master's hand. In the heavenly rank, Michael and Gabriel ministered as heaven's immediate connection to both the Early Rain to the Jews and the Latter Rain to the Gentiles. In both Early and Latter Rains, they occupy a season of three and one-half years. The Latter Rain is going to occupy the opening season of the last hour of Gentile times. In Early Rain times, the three and one-half years were the last half-week of the Jews' seventieth week of Daniel's prophecy. The *"two witnesses,"* Michael and Gabriel, have God's immediate mandate, with power.

"Days" are sun-reckoned and that pertains to the Church and the administration of Christ and grace. This *"thousand two hundred and threescore days"* is the same time slot as the forty-two months; they are coincidental. To wit: It is the ending season; nightfall of Gentile times. At the same time, it is the beginning, morning, of the Jewish dispensation headed by one hundred forty and four thousand sealed, believing Jews. That number is literal and not figurative. It is the administration referred to in Revelation 7:4: *"And I heard the number of them which were sealed: and there were sealed an hundred and forty and four thousand of all the tribes of the children of Israel."* The 'coincidental' aspect is spoken of in Isaiah 21:11–12, *". . . Watchman, what of the night? Watchman, what of the night? 12. The watchman said, the morning cometh, and also the night: if ye will enquire, enquire ye: return, come."*

In God's season, the sun will go down on the Gentiles; which season is the time frame of the first four horses: White, red, black, and pale; same as the four seals, declared by the first four trumpets. They will sound in the earth, and after three and one-half years, the Latter Rain will be finished. Thus ends the first four seals/trumpets; the heavenly mandate, declared by the trumpets, and the unto-mankind reporting, by the Church, of those orders. Four angels declare the opening of the first four seals. Evidenced is a Church having God's power. The intent: To judge by the declaration of the truth as manifest by the power to lay down their lives; martyrdom, and, thus, the overturning of any justification claimed by the Adamic, satanic world.

Repeating a principal precept: The wrath of God is manifest as a one-third portion. So being, there is this message: *"Come out of her, my people, that ye be not partakers of her sins, and that ye receive not of her plagues"* (Revelation 18:4). That is a concluding statement regarding the close of the Latter Rain church operation. Revelation 8:13 also gives a concluding statement: *"And I beheld, and heard an angel flying through the midst of heaven, saying with a loud voice, Woe, woe, woe, to the inhabiters of the earth by reason of the other voices of the trumpet of the three angels, which are yet to sound."*

The fifth seal opens the first of three woes. They are woes because the intermediary, daysman, to the Gentile world will cease. The Church will cease to function as the voice of reconciliation to a lost and dying world. Note: The word *'world'* is used as a collective, not persons, individuals, families, or groups. The Lord never turns away from a repentant soul. Going forward, the Church's mandate is finished.

VERSES 7–8: *7. "And when they shall have finished their testimony, the beast that ascendeth out of the bottomless pit shall make war against them, and shall overcome them, and kill them. 8. And their dead bodies shall lie in the street of the great city, which spiritually is called Sodom and Egypt, where also our Lord was crucified."*

Again, this *"beast that ascendeth out of the bottomless pit"* is the *"eighth"* and that equates to dramatically increased demon-possessed humanity. This juncture of moving forward from the Latter Rain being 'finished,' to the fifth seal/first woe is the initiation of a three-and-one-half year season of martyrdom.

Concerning the statement *"Sodom and Egypt, where our Lord was crucified,"* Sodom is a civilization defined by acts of sensual sin. *"Egypt"* can be considered as the societal and political opposition to God's divine will. This prophetic depiction portrays the present world and the soon coming world view of *"overcome them, and kill them."* Compelling sin is corrupting. And, sin, being commensurate with bad politics, gives 'evil' great power. Eventually, power to override mores and laws that otherwise protect the operation of the Church.

This brief treatment of the text is not comprehensive, but it is a consideration relating to the root and foundation of the anti-Christ evil where our Lord was crucified. It is this present and increasing *"Sodom and Egypt"* estate which equates to a break in God's protective hedge and gives satanic forces entry to possess certain of humanity.

VERSES 9–10: *9. "And they of the people and kindreds and tongues and nations shall see their dead bodies three days and an half, and shall not suffer their dead bodies to be put in graves. 10. And they that dwell upon the earth shall rejoice over them, and make merry, and shall send gifts one to another; because these two prophets tormented them that dwelt on the earth."*

This *"three days and an half"* equates to three and one-half years' time duration. It is the second half of a week of years, in which time frame, the Church operation is finished and the remanent of the Church is relegated to a place of standing-in-ridicule. The Church, having been mighty in godly works, will experience bloodshed. As in the time of Christ and the Early Church, a self-justifying world will remain 'unbelieving.' Martyrdom will be evidenced in the fashion of a society of earlier times; To wit: *". . . Herod the king stretched forth his hands to vex certain of the church. And he killed James the brother of John with the sword. And because he saw it pleased the Jews, he proceeded further to take Peter also . . ."* (Acts 12:1–3).

This mention of spirit-rank evil forces is a limited reality during the opening of the fifth seal/first woe. This mention, Revelation 11:7, is speaking from the "woes" aspect. Refreshing the statement: *"The beast that ascendeth out of the bottomless pit"* is the loosed demonic forces that God releases in full as the first woe progresses and allowed to rise to possess the selected rebellious of mankind. This is that first woe and occupies a three-and-one-half year season of martyrdom. It is 'allowed' of God. And, after the three and one-half years of martyrdom of the overcomers, the bride-remanent is completed. It is the *"until"* mentioned below. To wit: *"And when he had opened the fifth seal, I saw under the altar the souls of them that were slain for the word of God, and for the testimony which they held: And they cried with a loud voice, saying, How long, O Lord, holy and true, dost thou not judge and avenge our blood on them that dwell on the earth? And white robes were given unto every one of them; and it was said unto them, that they should rest yet for a little season, until their fellowservants also and their brethren, that should be killed as they were, should be fulfilled"* (Revelation 6:9–11).

This time of martyrdom is the season of God's just judgment of the eighth beast of Revelation 17:11. *"And the beast that was, and is not, even he is the eighth, and is of the seven, and goeth into perdition."* That part is mentioned with additional detail in Revelation 13:11–18. *11. "And I beheld another beast coming up out of the earth; and he had two horns like a lamb, and he spake as a dragon. 12. And he exerciseth all the power of the first beast before him, and causeth the earth and them which dwell therein to worship the first beast, whose deadly wound was healed. 13. And he doeth great wonders, so that he maketh fire come down from heaven on the earth in the sight of men, 14. And deceiveth them that dwell on the earth by the means of those miracles which he had power to do in the sight of the beast; saying to them that dwell on the earth, that they should make an image to the beast, which had the wound by a sword, and did live. 15. And he had power to give life unto the image of the beast, that the image of the beast should both speak, and cause that as many as would not worship the image of the beast should be killed. 16. And he causeth all, both small and great, rich and poor, free and bond, to receive a mark in their right hand, or in their foreheads: 17. And that no man might buy or sell, save he that had the mark, or the name of the beast, or the number of his name. 18. Here is wisdom. Let him that hath understanding count the number of the beast: for it is the number of a man; and his number is Six hundred threescore and six."*

VERSES 11–12: *11. "And after three days and an half the Spirit of life from God entered into them, and they stood upon their feet; and great fear fell upon them which saw them. 12. And they heard a great voice from heaven saying unto them, Come up hither. And they ascended up to heaven in a cloud; and their enemies beheld them."*

The *"two witnesses"* have God's immediate mandate, and that with power. On that point: God imputes, from heaven, unto his operatives that 'power.' Jesus had that power. He told his disciples, *"Therefore doth my Father love me, because I lay down my life, that I might take it again. No man taketh it from me, but I lay it down of myself. I have power to lay it down, and I have power to take it again. This commandment have I received of my Father"* (John 10:17–18). Jesus told Pilate, *"Thou couldest have no power at all against me, except it were given thee from above"* (John 19:11). Jesus, at the time of his departure into the heavens, stated, *"But ye shall receive power, after that the Holy Ghost is come upon you . . ."* (Acts 1:8). That power was of a spiritual kind, in the inner man; overcoming power, even unto death, and that is in the vein of Paul's statement, *"For if ye live after the flesh, ye shall die: but if ye through the Spirit do mortify the deeds of the body,* (death to the Adamic life) *ye shall live"* (Romans 8:13). This *"come up hither"* is the manifest 'power' of a literal resurrection. Paul stated concerning Jesus: *"And declared to be the Son of God with power, according to the spirit of holiness, by the resurrection from the dead"* (Romans 1:4). The Greek word *'dunamis,'* translated as 'power,' sometimes translate as 'miracles.'

VERSES 13–14: *13. "And the same hour was there a great earthquake, and the tenth part of the city fell, and in the earthquake were slain of men seven thousand: and the remnant were affrighted, and gave glory to the God of heaven. 14. The second woe is past; and, behold, the third woe cometh quickly."*

The end of the Gentile age is marked by the earthquake. The earthquake 'event' ends the first and second woes. Being more explicit, *"is past"* is the correct tense, being the earthquake is one of the sixth seal/second woe 'events,' The earthquake equates to a world war. Almost concurrent is the ascension. The millennium, day of the Lord, is arrived. The two sixth seal/second woe events are like the period at the end of a sentence. The Rapture, *"come up hither,"* initiates the seventh seal/third woe. Repeating: The Rapture and the earthquake events, totaling possibly six months, are not time-duration considerations; the events are heaven's declarations of 'endings' and 'beginnings.' The approximately six months given to the sixth seal/second woe fall within and at the end of the time frame of the three and one-half years of the fifth seal.

(Due consideration is given to the idea that the *"five months"* mentioned in Revelation 9:5, 10, is the *"short time"* of Revelation 12:12, and, that these five months would be immediately after, not within, the time frame of the first woe. The first part is an affirmative. The *"short time"* is likely *"five months."* The second part is not the 'timing' used in this writing. However, favoring that 'idea,' you might look at the 'last hour' as 15 years. That is: One day = a year. Then a year of days is 360 years/day. So that 1/24 of the 360 years would be 15 years. A bit convoluted, but acceptable to many. Using the last hour as 15 years and totaling the times: 3 ½ years + 3 ½ years + 5 months + 7 ½ years = 15 years. A month short, but acceptable using those calculations.)

Refreshing the point: This sixth seal/second woe are end-events of a few months; the Rapture marking the beginning of Christ's thousand-year reign and an earthquake/world war marking the end of Gentile times. Thus ends the sixth seal. The time of the seventh seal has arrived.

Now begins the millennial reign of Christ. It is the seventh seal/third woe. It is the up-front 7 ½ years of Christ's thousand-year reign. The seventh is seven; seven thunders, seven vials of plagues of the wrath of God, poured out into the earth.

(The rapture 'event' was not addressed in Revelation 6:12–17. To wit: *12. "And I beheld when he had opened the sixth seal, and, lo, there was a great earthquake; and the sun became black as sackcloth of hair, and the moon became as blood; 13. And the stars of heaven fell unto the earth, even as a fig tree casteth her untimely figs, when she is shaken of a mighty wind. 14. And the heaven departed as a scroll when it is rolled together; and every mountain and island were moved out of their places. 15. And the kings of the earth, and the great men, and the rich men, and the chief captains, and the mighty men, and every bondman, and every free man, hid themselves in the dens and in the rocks of the mountains; 16. And said to the mountains and rocks, Fall on us, and hide us from the face of him that sitteth on the throne, and from the wrath of the Lamb: 17. For the great day of his wrath is come; and who shall be able to stand?"*)

VERSES 15–19: *15. "And the seventh angel sounded; and there were great voices in heaven, saying, The kingdoms of this world are become the kingdoms of our Lord, and of his Christ; and he shall reign for ever and ever. 16. And the four and twenty elders, which sat before God on their seats, fell upon their faces, and worshipped God, 17. Saying, We give thee thanks, O Lord God Almighty, which art, and wast, and art to come; because thou hast taken to thee thy great power, and hast reigned. 18. And the nations were angry, and thy wrath is come, and the time of the dead, that they should be judged, and that thou shouldest give reward unto thy servants the prophets, and to the saints, and them that fear thy name, small and great; and shouldest destroy them which destroy the earth. 19. And the temple of God was opened in heaven, and there was seen in his temple the ark of his testament: and there were lightnings, and voices, and thunderings, and an earthquake, and great hail."*

At this point in time, the seventh seal/third woe is opened. As per the 'Jericho' similitude, the seventh is sevenfold. It is the beginning of the millennium day of the Lord; the season of seven and one-half years of the seven vials and the seven thunders. The conclusion of this third woe being the Armageddon 'event.' From a technical standpoint, the seventh seal is a 'fullness' or 'completed' concept; meaning that the seventh, which is the day of the Lord, is a continuing era of purging unto a perfect day. As said in Revelation 21:4, *"The former things are passed away."* Again, the front end of that day is God's purging seven vials of wrath. Immediately predating the beginning of the 'Lord's Day,' before God's wrath is poured out, the elect will be caught up to heaven. Thus begins the 'Hebron' marriage event. Knowing the sequence of events is understanding the validity of a 'pre-Trib rapture.'

REFRESHING THE TIMELINE, CHAPTER 11, we note that concurrently, during the time of the first four seals/horses and including the fifth seal/first woe, the Gentile worlds are judged and concluded. The sun goes down on the Gentile world. Isaiah 21:12 also states *"and also the night."* And, the Lord has gained 'product;' both terrestrial and celestial, the remnant of the very elect, *"caught up to God, and to his throne."* That is, *"ascended up to heaven in a cloud"* (Revelation 12:5; 11:12).

Concerning 'product: The book of Revelation places chapter 7 between the sixth seal/second woe and the seventh seal/third woe. Chapter 7 is perfectly placed. It reveals the 'products' of the seals being opened. One product is 144,000 Jews being sealed, in Christ, for the purpose of the terrestrial administration, geography-related, for the upcoming day of the Lord. The terrestrial part is given in the first eight verses of the chapter. To wit: Revelation 7:1–8. *1. "And after these things I saw four angels standing on the four corners of the earth, holding the four winds of the earth, that the wind should not blow on the earth, nor on the sea, nor on any tree. 2. And I saw another angel ascending from the east, having the seal of the living God: and he cried with a loud voice to the four angels, to whom it was given to hurt the earth and the sea, 3. Saying, Hurt not the earth, neither the sea, nor the trees, till we have sealed the servants of our God in their foreheads. 4. And I heard the number of them which were sealed: and there were sealed an hundred and forty and four thousand of all the tribes of the children of Israel. 5. Of the tribe of Judah were sealed twelve thousand. Of the tribe of Reuben were sealed twelve thousand. Of the tribe of Gad were sealed twelve thousand. 6. Of the tribe of Aser were sealed twelve thousand. Of the tribe of Nepthalim were sealed twelve thousand. Of the tribe of Manasses were sealed twelve thousand. 7. Of the tribe of Simeon were sealed twelve thousand. Of the tribe of Levi were sealed twelve thousand. Of the tribe of Issachar were sealed twelve thousand. 8. Of the tribe of Zabulon were sealed twelve thousand. Of the tribe of Joseph were sealed twelve thousand. Of the tribe of Benjamin were sealed twelve thousand."* Treating this terrestrial product, Isaiah 21:12 states the *"morning cometh."* On the Jew part, it is the declaration that God's promises to the Jews is definitely, decidedly, wonderfully, going to happen. The promises to Abraham and his descendants are geography-based. The sun will arise for them. They are going to be married to the land. The 'bride' message of Isaiah 62:4: *"Thou shalt no more be termed Forsaken; neither shall thy land any more be termed Desolate: but thou shalt be called Hephzibah, and thy land Beulah: for the Lord delighteth in thee, and thy land shall be married."* So be it: What God has joined together, let no man put asunder. It is signed, sealed, and settled, in the time of the first five seals, concluding with the event of the sixth seal. Jumping ahead, the conclusion of that determination will happen at the conclusion of the third woe. That is, the Armageddon war event, when Jesus returns to take Jerusalem for his own.

Concurrently, another 'product' is the completing of the 144,000 very elect, called to the throne of God. That is the 'high-water mark' of resurrection doctrinal understanding. Those occupying a celestial estate, granted immortality, and ruling and reigning in a heavenly realm with Christ for a thousand years. Revelation 7:9–17 describes the estate of the 'product' of God's "finished" celestial. To wit: *9. After this I beheld, and, lo, a great multitude, which no man could number, of all nations, and kindreds, and people, and tongues, stood before the throne, and before the Lamb, clothed with white robes, and palms in their hands; 10. And cried with a loud voice, saying, Salvation to our God which sitteth upon the throne, and unto the Lamb. 11. And all the angels stood round about the throne, and about the elders and the four beasts, and fell before the throne on their faces, and worshipped God, 12. Saying, Amen: Blessing, and glory, and wisdom, and thanksgiving, and honour, and power, and might, be unto our God for ever and ever. Amen. 13. And one of the elders answered, saying unto me, What are these which are arrayed in white robes? and whence came they? 14. And I said unto him, Sir, thou knowest. And he said to me, These are they which came out of great tribulation, and have washed their robes, and made them white in the blood of the Lamb. 15. Therefore are they before the throne of God, and serve him day and night in his temple: and he that sitteth on the throne shall dwell among them. 16. They shall hunger no more, neither thirst any more; neither shall the sun light on them, nor any heat. 17. For the Lamb which is in the midst of the throne shall feed them, and shall lead them unto living fountains of waters: and God shall wipe away all tears from their eyes.* These are those spoken of in Revelation 11:12, *"They ascended up to heaven."*

CHAPTER XII

REVELATION, CHAPTERS 12-13

CHAPTER 12: *1. "And there appeared a great wonder in heaven; a woman clothed with the sun, and the moon under her feet, and upon her head a crown of twelve stars: 2. And she being with child cried, travailing in birth, and pained to be delivered. 3. And there appeared another wonder in heaven; and behold a great red dragon, having seven heads and ten horns, and seven crowns upon his heads. 4. And his tail drew the third part of the stars of heaven, and did cast them to the earth: and the dragon stood before the woman which was ready to be delivered, for to devour her child as soon as it was born. 5. And she brought forth a man child, who was to rule all nations with a rod of iron: and her child was caught up unto God, and to his throne. 6. And the woman fled into the wilderness, where she hath a place prepared of God, that they should feed her there a thousand two hundred and threescore days. 7. And there was war in heaven: Michael and his angels fought against the dragon; and the dragon fought and his angels, 8. And prevailed not; neither was their place found any more in heaven. 9. And the great dragon was cast out, that old serpent, called the Devil, and Satan, which deceiveth the whole world: he was cast out into the earth, and his angels were cast out with him. 10. And I heard a loud voice saying in heaven, Now is come salvation, and strength, and the kingdom of our God, and the power of his Christ: for the accuser of our brethren is cast down, which accused them before our God day and night. 11. And they overcame him by the blood of the Lamb, and by the word of their testimony; and they loved not their lives unto the death. 12. Therefore rejoice, ye heavens, and ye that dwell in them. Woe to the inhabiters of the earth and of the sea! for the devil is come down unto you, having great wrath, because he knoweth that he hath but a short time. 13. And when the dragon saw that he was cast unto the earth, he persecuted the woman which brought forth the man child. 14. And to the woman were given two wings of a great eagle, that she might fly into the wilderness, into her place, where she is nourished for a time, and times, and half a time, from the face of the serpent. 15. And the serpent cast out of his mouth water as a flood after the woman, that he might cause her to be carried away of the flood. 16. And the earth helped the woman, and the earth opened her mouth, and swallowed up the flood which the dragon cast out of his mouth. 17. And the dragon was wroth with the woman, and went to make war with the remnant of her seed, which keep the commandments of God, and have the testimony of Jesus Christ."*

Chapter 12 describes the events of the sixth seal/second woe. The time of the sixth seal/second woe falls primarily within the latter months of the three and one-half years allotted to the fifth seal. Verses 1 through 5 depict the travail, the satanic opposition, and the Rapture of the man-child. These five verses give a sort of up-front synopsis of what the whole chapter is reporting. The remaining verses give an overview of the persecution of the church and the remanent church. This chapter portrays the persecution and product of the church. It is the conclusion of the *"little season"* of martyrdom that begun with the fifth seal/first woe.

VERSES 1–4: *1. "And there appeared a great wonder in heaven; a woman clothed with the sun, and the moon under her feet, and upon her head a crown of twelve stars: 2. And she being with child cried, travailing in birth, and pained to be delivered 3. And there appeared another wonder in heaven; and behold a great red dragon, having seven heads and ten horns, and seven crowns upon his heads. 4. And his tail drew the third part of the stars of heaven, and did cast them to the earth: and the dragon stood before the woman which was ready to be delivered, for to devour her child as soon as it was born.*

The *"great wonder in heaven"* is heaven's depiction of Christ's Church. The child about to be born is the product of the two-thousand-year church age. The nation of Israel cannot claim this estate of *"clothed with the sun, and the moon under her feet."* That would be tantamount to being clothed in the grace of Christ and having fulfilled the Law. Only the Church of which Christ is the head fulfills that estate. God's intent and desire toward this precious fruit of the earth: *"Behold, the husbandman waiteth for the precious fruit of the earth, and hath long patience for it, until he receive the early and latter rain"* (James 5:7). Jesus identified the husbandman, stating, *"I am the true vine, and my Father is the husbandman"* (John 15:1).

The term *"another wonder in heaven"* in verse 3, brings to mind Paul's statement to the Corinthians, *"the mystery of iniquity."* Here we see the dragon. He is red; operative both in the earth realm and in the spirit realm. The time frame is the fifth seal/first woe. It is the end-season of the martyrdom of the saints. Certain of fallen humanity are devil-possessed. The man of sin entertains the devil himself. So being, the murdering of the saints will judge both the heaven and the earth. Jesus' death bruised the serpent's head.

Pertaining to the 'order' of anti-Christ on earth, it was Martin Luther that wielded the sword of the Word of God: *"The Just shall live by faith."* That wounding of the beast is being healed. God is allowing it to happen, as unto-final-judgment. To wit: So that the death of the saints will be the second witness that judges the matter. The dragon is the spirit and author of iniquity against God. Human government will 'register' with it. The dragon and civil power become a unity. The dragon authored the civilizations of Egypt, Assyria, Babylon, Persia, Greece, and Rome; add modern Rome, emblematic of the presently arising anti-Christ world government. Seven heads and seven crowns of powers. *"Ten horns"* will soon be evident. *"And the ten horns which thou sawest are ten kings, which have received no kingdom as yet; but receive power as kings one hour with the beast"* (Revelation 17:12). Thus, we see the coming estate of civil power as 'the dragon.' Verse 4 says, *"His tail drew a third part of the stars of heaven, and did cast them to the earth."* More detail will follow in the chapter. The dragon powers will not be able to stop the Church or hinder its two-thousand-year production. Jesus' words, *"The gates of hell shall not prevail against it."*

Timewise, this celestial product preempts the final terrestrial product. See Micah 5:3. *"Therefore will he give them up, until the time that she which travaileth hath brought forth: then the remnant of his brethren shall return unto the children of Israel."* This *"give them up"* is a two-thousand-year pause while the chosen people of Israel dwell in spiritual darkness. It is likened unto death, where there is no time consideration. Paul dedicated the eleventh chapter of Romans to the matter. Especially, see Romans 11:25. *"For I would not, brethren, that ye should be ignorant of this mystery, lest ye should be wise in your own conceits; that blindness in part is hap-*

pened to Israel, until the fullness of the Gentiles be come in." The Old Testament Scripture we subscribe to is Hosea 6:1, 2. *1. "Come, and let us return unto the Lord: for he hath torn, and he will heal us; he hath smitten, and he will bind us up. 2. After two days will he revive us: in the third day he will raise us up, and we shall live in his sight."* The two days are taken to be two thousand years. This two-day pause is generally thought to be from the stoning of Stephen till the Rapture. Again, consider Micah 5:3, *"Therefore will he give them up, until the time that she which travaileth hath brought forth: then the remnant of his brethren shall return unto the children of Israel."*

Regarding the 'temptation' to set a time for the Lord's return: The starting point of the two thousand years, two days, of Gentile times is generally thought to be the same as the endpoint of the Jew's allotted four hundred ninety years, seventy weeks of years, Daniel 9:24. That endpoint is the stoning of Stephen about AD 33. Adding two thousand years, the return of Christ, beginning the day of the Lord, would be about AD 2033. This writer cannot justify us putting God in this 'box' of prognosticating. The beginning of Gentile times could have started any time in the approximately forty years dying-time of the Jewish nation. That is, AD 30 to AD 70. That is, using the AD 30 crucifixion of Jesus till the destruction of Jerusalem; covering the Spiritual death, and then, on to the death of the Nation.

Regarding the 'product' of the Church that reflects the celestial part: See Revelation 14:1, 3. *1. "And I looked, and lo, a Lamb stood on the mount Sion, and with him an hundred forty and four thousand, having his Father's name written in their foreheads . . . 3. And they sung as it were a new song before the throne, and before the four beasts, and the elders: and no man could learn that song but the hundred and forty and four thousand, which were redeemed from the earth."* We say, the song of Moses and the Lamb. That is per Revelation 15:3: *"And they sing the song of Moses the servant of God, and the song of the Lamb, saying, Great and marvelous are thy works, Lord God Almighty, just and true are thy ways, thou King of saints."*

The following verses, 5 through 9, are the events of the sixth seal/second woe; including opening the seventh seal/third woe. The two sixth seal events fall within the time frame of the fifth seal.

VERSES 5–9: *5. "And she brought forth a man child, who was to rule all nations with a rod of iron: and her child was caught up unto God, and to his throne. 6. And the woman fled into the wilderness, where she hath a place prepared of God, that they should feed her there a thousand two hundred and threescore days. 7. And there was war in heaven: Michael and his angels fought against the dragon; and the dragon fought and his angels, 8. And prevailed not; neither was their place found any more in heaven. 9. And the great dragon was cast out, that old serpent, called the Devil, and Satan, which deceiveth the whole world: he was cast out into the earth, and his angels were cast out with him."*

The Church will produce the man-child, being *"caught up unto God."* His estate of rulership is established. The seven-and-one-half-year marriage supper of the Lamb sees the *"man child"* graduate to *"the bride, the Lamb's wife."* Post-Rapture, the remanent church will flee into the wilderness for a period of three and one-half years. That *"place"* is God's 'prescription.' That is geographic and includes angelic protections. It is not 'happenstance.' The *"war in heaven"* is not a battle of shields and swords. It is a battle of 'justification' of the saints and our Lord and our God, versus the 'accusations' of the wicked one. *"To declare, I say, at this time his righteousness: that he might be just, and the justifier of him which believeth in Jesus"* (Romans 3:26). God wins. *"He was cast out into the earth, and his angels were cast out with him."* Later stated, *"The accuser of our brethren is cast down."* The devil being cast out of heaven initiates the *"silence in heaven about the space of half an hour"* (Revelation 8:1).

Verses 10 through 13 begin the seventh seal/third woe. It occupies the first seven and one-half years of Christ's millennium reign. Repeating: Satan is cast out and there is *"silence in heaven about the space of half an hour."* The half an hour being seven and one-half years.

VERSES 10–13: *10. "And I heard a loud voice saying in heaven, Now is come salvation, and strength, and the kingdom of our God, and the power of his Christ: for the accuser of our brethren is cast down, which accused them before our God day and night. 11. And they overcame him by the blood of the Lamb, and by the word of their testimony; and they loved not their lives unto the death. 12. Therefore rejoice, ye heavens, and ye that dwell in them. Woe to the inhabiters of the earth and of the sea! for the devil is come down unto you, having great wrath, because he knoweth that he hath but a short time. 13. And when the dragon saw that he was cast unto the earth, he persecuted the woman which brought forth the man child."*

Verse 10 is a declaration from heaven. It is the detail of the previous verses. The tenth verse refers to the beginning of *"the kingdom of our God"* which equates to the millennium reign of Christ. The beginning of the seventh angel/third woe. It is the Lord's Day and he is the victor. It is the time when the remanent Church, having produced the man-child, and the Jewish leadership 144,000 strong, become unified in one; totally and completely *"finished."* That is the fullness of Scripture spoken by Paul. *"For he is our peace, who hath made both one, and hath broken down the middle wall of partition between us; . . . And that he might reconcile both unto God in one body by the cross, having slain the enmity thereby . . . In whom ye also are builded together for an habitation of God through the Spirit"* (Ephesians 2:14, 16, 22).

VERSES 14–17: *14. "And to the woman were given two wings of a great eagle, that she might fly into the wilderness, into her place, where she is nourished for a time, and times, and half a time, from the face of the serpent. 15. And the serpent cast out of his mouth water as a flood after the woman, that he might cause her to be carried away of the flood. 16. And the earth helped the woman, and the earth opened her mouth, and swallowed up the flood which the dragon cast out of his mouth. 17. And the dragon was wroth with the woman, and went to make war with the remnant of her seed, which keep the commandments of God, and have the testimony of Jesus Christ."*

This mention of the *"woman"* being saved and the time frame of three and one-half years, is likely the same as mentioned previously in verse 6. If it is a second three-and-one-half year happening, that would open up the possibility of events transpiring at the midpoint of the third woe. That 'possibility' is an unknown and will not be treated. The *"woman"* of verse 6 and verse 14 are seen as the same. Beginning with verse 10, we have the heavenly declaration, including a repeat of the detail of verse 6. The picture here of the woman being *"given two wings of a great eagle"* does favor the idea that, in the last hour of Gentile times, the remanent church, Jew and Gentile worldwide, will gravitate to the Middle East and unite with the remanent Jew and remanent church. Thenceforth fled together. To wit: *"And ye shall flee to the valley of the mountains; for the valley of the mountains shall reach unto Azal: yea, ye shall flee, like as ye fled from before the earthquake in the days of Uzziah king of Judah; and the Lord my God shall come, and all the saints with thee"* (Zechariah 14:5). A "flood" is the serpent's manner. Isaiah 59:19 states, *". . . When the enemy shall come in like a flood, the Spirit of the Lord shall lift up a standard against him."* Isaiah's statement may be both spiritual and literal. The 'spiritual' is usually complemented with naturally occurring phenomena. This escape to safety includes geological phenomena and the Zechariah 14 passage supports that viewpoint. The statements of the last verse of this twelfth chapter are predictable and the net effect is also. God's will and keeping-power prevail. The serpent's *"war with the remnant of her seed"* is initiated, in the earth, post-Rapture.

CHAPTER 13: *1. "And I stood upon the sand of the sea, and saw a beast rise up out of the sea, having seven heads and ten horns, and upon his horns ten crowns, and upon his heads the name of blasphemy. 2. And the beast which I saw was like unto a leopard, and his feet were as the feet of a bear, and his mouth as the mouth of a lion: and the dragon gave him his power, and his seat, and great authority. 3. And I saw one of his heads as it were wounded to death; and his deadly wound was healed: and all the world wondered after the beast. 4. And they worshipped the dragon which gave power unto the beast: and they worshipped the beast, saying, Who is like unto the beast? who is able to make war with him? 5. And there was given unto him a mouth speaking great things and blasphemies; and power was given unto him to continue forty and two months. 6. And he opened his mouth in blasphemy against God, to blaspheme his name, and his tabernacle, and them that dwell in heaven. 7. And it was given unto him to make war with the saints, and to overcome them: and power was given him over all kindreds, and tongues, and nations. 8. And all that dwell upon the earth shall worship him, whose names are not written in the book of life of the Lamb slain from the foundation of the world. 9. If any man have an ear, let him hear. 10. He that leadeth into captivity shall go into captivity: he that killeth with the sword must be killed with the sword. Here is the patience and the faith of the saints. 11. And I beheld another beast coming up out of the earth; and he had two horns like a lamb, and he spake as a dragon. 12. And he exerciseth all the power of the first beast before him, and causeth the earth and them which dwell therein to worship the first beast, whose deadly wound was healed. 13. And he doeth great wonders, so that he maketh fire come down from heaven on the earth in the sight of men, 14. And deceiveth them that dwell on the earth by the means of those miracles which he had power to do in the sight of the beast; saying to them that dwell on the earth, that they should make an image to the beast, which had the wound by a sword, and did live. 15. And he had power to give life unto the image of the beast, that the image of the beast should both speak, and cause that as many as would not worship the image of the beast should be killed. 16. And he causeth all, both small and great, rich and poor, free and bond, to receive a mark in their right hand, or in their foreheads: 17. And that no man might buy or sell, save he that had the mark, or the name of the beast, or the number of his name. 18. Here is wisdom. Let him that hath understanding count the number of the beast: for it is the number of a man; and his number is Six hundred threescore and six."*

Chapter 13 occupies the second three-and-one-half year period following the Latter Rain. In total, it is the forty-two months *"little season"* of martyrdom of the saints.

VERSES 1–10: *1 "And I stood upon the sand of the sea, and saw a beast rise up out of the sea, having seven heads and ten horns, and upon his horns ten crowns, and upon his heads the name of blasphemy. 2. And the beast which I saw was like unto a leopard, and his feet were as the feet of a bear, and his mouth as the mouth of a lion: and the dragon gave him his power, and his seat, and great authority. 3. And I saw one of his heads as it were wounded to death; and his deadly wound was healed: and all the world wondered after the beast. 4. And they worshipped the dragon which gave power unto the beast: and they worshipped the beast, saying, Who is like unto the beast? who is able to make war with him? 5. And there was given unto him a mouth speaking great things and blasphemies; and power was given unto him to continue forty and two months. 6. And he opened his mouth in blasphemy against God, to blaspheme his name, and his tabernacle, and them that dwell in heaven. 7. And it was given unto him to make war with the saints, and to overcome them: and power was given him over all kindreds, and tongues, and nations. 8. And all that dwell upon the earth shall worship him, whose names are not written in the book of life of the Lamb slain from the foundation of the world. 9. If any man have an ear, let him hear. 10. He that leadeth into captivity shall go into captivity: he that killeth with the sword must be killed with the sword. Here is the patience and the faith of the saints."*

From the onset, the three-and-one-half year ministry, *"testimony,"* of the Latter Rain church was *"finished."* John is now given the detailed *"little season"* of martyrdom and the resulting setting forth of the judgment of the Gentile world, including sealing the judgment of the dragon.

"The sea" gives rise to a *"beast."* Like *"the waters,"* it involves *"peoples, and multitudes, and nations, and tongues"* (Revelation 17:15). Beyond the 'masses,' it arises with a definitive motive and leadership. It is anti-Christ. Starting with Egypt, seven world powers have exercised dominion over God's righteous line. The seven are Egypt, Assyria, Babylon, Persia, Greece, pagan Rome, and religious Rome. Presently four are viable. As per the seventh chapter of Daniel: Babylon, the *"lion;"* presently Iraq. Persia, the *"bear;"* presently Iran. Greece, the *"leopard."* Alexander the Great, preempting 'geography,' is morphed to be the *"iron"* of Roman power. Rome's power is both civil and religious; *"dreadful and terrible, and strong exceedingly."* If a duality of interpretation is brought to bear, we can reasonably see the modern-day, non-Middle East compliment as the *"lion"* being Britain, the *"eagle"* being America, as integrated with Britain, the *"bear"* being Russia, and the *"leopard"* being Germany. The *"fourth beast"* being Rome. Even till the *"little horn"* of universal papal-Roman persuasion; the *"iron"* of civil and religious. The seventh-of-seven beast of Revelation 13, wounded and then healed, is allowed by God to dominate the religious scene and persecute the Church. *"Power was given unto him to continue forty and two months."* The beast, empowered by the dragon, destroys and murders the Church. Repeating: Thus begins the time of the fifth seal/first woe; martyrdom of certain of the Church, being Christ's body and the second witness.

VERSES 13:11–18: *11. "And I beheld another beast coming up out of the earth; and he had two horns like a lamb, and he spake as a dragon. 12. And he exerciseth all the power of the first beast before him, and causeth the earth and them which dwell therein to worship the first beast, whose deadly wound was healed. 13. And he doeth great wonders, so that he maketh fire come down from heaven on the earth in the sight of men, 14. And deceiveth them that dwell on the earth by the means of those miracles which he had power to do in the sight of the beast; saying to them that dwell on the earth, that they should make an image to the beast, which had the wound by a sword, and did live. 15. And he had power to give life unto the image of the beast, that the image of the beast should both speak, and cause that as many as would not worship the image of the beast should be killed. 16. And he causeth all, both small and great, rich and poor, free and bond, to receive a mark in their right hand, or in their foreheads: 17. And that no man might buy or sell, save he that had the mark, or the name of the beast, or the number of his name. 18. Here is wisdom. Let him that hath understanding count the number of the beast: for it is the number of a man; and his number is Six hundred threescore and six."*

Included in the time frame of the fifth seal, John sees *"another beast coming up out of the earth."* It is an *"image"* of the seventh. It is *"the eighth"* of Revelation 17:11. This system has appeal to 'religious spirits,' having a lamb-like appearance. It is a dragon. The statement *"spake as a dragon,"* lets us know that the demonic spirits have moved, or been moved, to 'possession' of men and not just impression, repression, and suppression. This graduation from seventh to eighth is *"another beast coming up out of the earth."* Religious spirits having the mindset of the beast will be overcome and persuaded by the powers of the dragon. That is, people *"whose names are not written in the book of life of the Lamb,"* the ones having *"the mark, or the name of the beast, or the number of his name."* This would include humanity falling into the category of *"way side"* soil. *"When any one heareth the word of the kingdom, and understandeth it not, then cometh the wicked one, and catcheth away that which was sown in his heart. This is he which receiveth seed by the way side"* (Matthew 13:4, 19).

The end-time world will be further subjected to oversight and control afforded by advanced technology. Given the 'personal' estate of the satanic order; spirit, soul, and body, it is a six, six, six.

CHAPTER XIII

REVELATION, CHAPTERS 14-16

CHAPTER 14: *1. "And I looked, and, lo, a Lamb stood on the mount Sion, and with him an hundred forty and four thousand, having his Father's name written in their foreheads. 2. And I heard a voice from heaven, as the voice of many waters, and as the voice of a great thunder: and I heard the voice of harpers harping with their harps: 3. And they sung as it were a new song before the throne, and before the four beasts, and the elders: and no man could learn that song but the hundred and forty and four thousand, which were redeemed from the earth. 4. These are they which were not defiled with women; for they are virgins. These are they which follow the Lamb whithersoever he goeth. These were redeemed from among men, being the firstfruits unto God and to the Lamb. 5. And in their mouth was found no guile: for they are without fault before the throne of God. 6. And I saw another angel fly in the midst of heaven, having the everlasting gospel to preach unto them that dwell on the earth, and to every nation, and kindred, and tongue, and people, 7. Saying with a loud voice, Fear God, and give glory to him; for the hour of his judgment is come: and worship him that made heaven, and earth, and the sea, and the fountains of waters. 8. And there followed another angel, saying, Babylon is fallen, is fallen, that great city, because she made all nations drink of the wine of the wrath of her fornication. 9. And the third angel followed them, saying with a loud voice, If any man worship the beast and his image, and receive his mark in his forehead, or in his hand, 10. The same shall drink of the wine of the wrath of God, which is poured out without mixture into the cup of his indignation; and he shall be tormented with fire and brimstone in the presence of the holy angels, and in the presence of the Lamb: 11. And the smoke of their torment ascendeth up for ever and ever: and they have no rest day nor night, who worship the beast and his image, and whosoever receiveth the mark of his name. 12. Here is the patience of the saints: here are they that keep the commandments of God, and the faith of Jesus. 13. And I heard a voice from heaven saying unto me, Write, Blessed are the dead which die in the Lord from henceforth: Yea, saith the Spirit, that they may rest from their labors; and their works do follow them. 14. And I looked, and behold a white cloud, and upon the cloud one sat like unto the Son of man, having on his head a golden crown, and in his hand a sharp sickle. 15. And another angel came out of the temple, crying with a loud voice to him that sat on the cloud, Thrust in thy sickle, and reap: for the time is come for thee to reap; for the harvest of the earth is ripe. 16. And he that sat on the cloud thrust in his sickle on the earth; and the earth was reaped. 17. And another angel came out of the temple which is in heaven, he also having a sharp sickle. 18. And another angel came out from the altar, which had power over fire; and cried with a loud cry to him that had the sharp sickle, saying, Thrust in thy sharp sickle, and gather the clusters of the vine of the earth; for her grapes are fully ripe. 19. And the angel thrust in his sickle into the earth, and gathered the vine of the earth, and cast it into the great winepress of the wrath of God. 20. And the winepress was trodden without the city, and blood came out of the winepress, even unto the horse bridles, by the space of a thousand and six hundred furlongs."*

It is the time of the seventh seal/third woe. The events of the sixth seal/second woe have passed and the man-child is before the throne.

VERSES 1–5: *1. "And I looked, and, lo, a Lamb stood on the mount Sion, and with him an hundred forty and four thousand, having his Father's name written in their foreheads. 2. And I heard a voice from heaven, as the voice of many waters, and as the voice of a great thunder: and I heard the voice of harpers harping with their harps: 3. And they sung as it were a new song before the throne, and before the four beasts, and the elders: and no man could learn that song but the hundred and forty and four thousand, which were redeemed from the earth. 4. These are they which were not defiled with women; for they are virgins. These are they which follow the Lamb whithersoever he goeth. These were redeemed from among men, being the firstfruits unto God and to the Lamb. 5. And in their mouth was found no guile: for they are without fault before the throne of God."*

Chapter 14 reveals the glorious high-calling 'product.' Their 'finished' estate is the accomplishment of the first and second woes. The glorious performing of God's plan of salvation and rewarding the saints.

The 'redeemed' portrayed here is to the glory of God. The promise of the Lord's return did not fail. As saith the Scripture: *"And while they looked steadfastly toward heaven as he went up, behold, two men stood by them in white apparel; Which also said, Ye men of Galilee, why stand ye gazing up into heaven? this same Jesus, which is taken up from you into heaven, shall so come in like manner as ye have seen him go into heaven"* (Acts 1:10–11). *"And his feet shall stand in that day upon the mount of Olives, which is before Jerusalem on the east"* (Zechariah 14:4).

The host of 144,000 is the same as the *"caught up"* man-child. The "marriage supper of the Lamb" will see the host graduate to *"the bride, the Lamb's wife."* The 'event' of the Armageddon war concludes the seventh vial, ending the season of the *"marriage supper of the Lamb."* The setting is heaven. They are before the throne, the four living creature and the elders. They sing the song of Moses and the Lamb. This host are overcomers, perfected, 'finished.'

Beginning with verse 6, the declaration of the Lord's Day goes forth, including the judgment of the false prophet and the beast. To wit:

VERSES 6–11: *6. "And I saw another angel fly in the midst of heaven, having the everlasting gospel to preach unto them that dwell on the earth, and to every nation, and kindred, and tongue, and people, 7. Saying with a loud voice, Fear God, and give glory to him; for the hour of his judgment is come: and worship him that made heaven, and earth, and the sea, and the fountains of waters. 8. And there followed another angel, saying, Babylon is fallen, is fallen, that great city, because she made all nations drink of the wine of the wrath of her fornication. 9. And the third angel followed them, saying with a loud voice, If any man worship the beast and his image, and receive his mark in his forehead, or in his hand, 10. The same shall drink of the wine of the wrath of God, which is poured out without mixture into the cup of his indignation; and he shall be tormented with fire and brimstone in the presence of the holy angels, and in the presence of the Lamb: 11. And the smoke of their torment ascendeth up for ever and ever: and they have no rest day nor night, who worship the beast and his image, and whosoever receiveth the mark of his name."*

Scripture plainly states the matter. Three angels declare God's righteous judgment on the earth and peoples, the beast, Babylon, and those numbered as worshipping the beast having his mark in their forehead or hand: *"For the hour of his judgment is come."*

VERSES 12–16: *12. "Here is the patience of the saints: here are they that keep the commandments of God, and the faith of Jesus. 13. And I heard a voice from heaven saying unto me, Write, Blessed are the dead which die in the Lord from henceforth: Yea, saith the Spirit, that they may rest from their labors; and their works do follow them. 14. And I looked, and behold a white cloud, and upon the cloud one sat like unto the Son of man, having on his head a golden crown, and in his hand a sharp sickle. 15. And another angel came out of the temple, crying with a loud voice to him that sat on the cloud, Thrust in thy sickle, and reap: for the time is come for thee to reap; for the harvest of the earth is ripe. 16. And he that sat on the cloud thrust in his sickle on the earth; and the earth was reaped."*

In both verse 2 and verse 13, the *"voice from heaven"* addresses the estate and blessing of those that keep God's commandments. This first reaping, verse 15, pertains to the blessed of the Lord. Repeating: Indeed, they are under the purview of the *"voice from heaven."* It is *"the harvest of the earth,"* the voice of the Lord, *"the Son of man,"* the same as *"a voice from heaven."*

Consider the symbolism reflected in this fourteenth chapter: The voice from heaven is Christ, the main post and candle. He is shown to be the 'because of him,' or *"by him"* voice of God. First the 'hidden' wisdom of God, and then the 'revealed' wisdom of God. And, like the candlestick, there are six angels who further enlighten. That is, verses 6, 8, 9, 15, and the following verses 17 and 18. The four living creatures carry the same glorious reflection of Christ.

VERSES 17–20: *17. "And another angel came out of the temple which is in heaven, he also having a sharp sickle. 18. And another angel came out from the altar, which had power over fire; and cried with a loud cry to him that had the sharp sickle, saying, Thrust in thy sharp sickle, and gather the clusters of the vine of the earth; for her grapes are fully ripe. 19. And the angel thrust in his sickle into the earth, and gathered the vine of the earth, and cast it into the great winepress of the wrath of God. 20. And the winepress was trodden without the city, and blood came out of the winepress, even unto the horse bridles, by the space of a thousand and six hundred furlongs."*

These concluding verses of the fourteenth chapter reveal the wrath of God on the earth and the beast. The false prophet is not mentioned here, but the proponents of the false prophet are mentioned. The false prophet has the mind of Satan and his proponents do likewise. They are marked because they do his works and have his mindset. The revealing of judgment is shown clearly in the text.

Repeating: Seven angels ministered in this fourteenth chapter. *"A voice from heaven"* is mentioned in verse 2 and in verse 13. Both times the voice addresses the 'blessed.' That voice is one angel. Christ. Reasonably, because the first *"angel,"* mentioned as such in verse 6, is addressed as *"another angel."*

CHAPTER 15: *1. "And I saw another sign in heaven, great and marvelous, seven angels having the seven last plagues; for in them is filled up the wrath of God. 2. And I saw as it were a sea of glass mingled with fire: and them that had gotten the victory over the beast, and over his image, and over his mark, and over the number of his name, stand on the sea of glass, having the harps of God. 3. And they sing the song of Moses the servant of God, and the song of the Lamb, saying, Great and marvelous are thy works, Lord God Almighty; just and true are thy ways, thou King of saints. 4. Who shall not fear thee, O Lord, and glorify thy name? for thou only art holy: for all nations shall come and worship before thee; for thy judgments are made manifest. 5. And after that I looked, and, behold, the temple of the tabernacle of the testimony in heaven was opened: 6. And the seven angels came out of the temple, having the seven plagues, clothed in pure and white linen, and having their breasts girded with golden girdles. 7. And one of the four beasts gave unto the seven angels seven golden vials full of the wrath of God, who liveth for ever and ever. 8. And the temple was filled with smoke from the glory of God, and from his power; and no man was able to enter into the temple, till the seven plagues of the seven angels were fulfilled."*

It is the time of the seventh seal/third woe. The high-calling host is stationed in heaven. The wrath of God goes forth; the seven and one-half years of seven vials and seven plagues.

Touching similitudes, the time of 'Hebron' has arrived, and the taking of Jerusalem is just seven and one-half years into the future. Referencing that event: *"And David danced before the Lord with all his might; and David was girded with a linen ephod. So David and all the house of Israel brought up the ark of the Lord with shouting, and with the sound of the trumpet"* (II Samuel 6:14–15). This glorious event was in the time of transitioning from Hebron to Jerusalem.

VERSES 1–4: *1 "And I saw another sign in heaven, great and marvelous, seven angels having the seven last plagues; for in them is filled up the wrath of God. 2. And I saw as it were a sea of glass mingled with fire: and them that had gotten the victory over the beast, and over his image, and over his mark, and over the number of his name, stand on the sea of glass, having the harps of God. 3. And they sing the song of Moses the servant of God, and the song of the Lamb, saying, Great and marvelous are thy works, Lord God Almighty; just and true are thy ways, thou King of saints. 4. Who shall not fear thee, O Lord, and glorify thy name? for thou only art holy: for all nations shall come and worship before thee; for thy judgments are made manifest."*

Chapter 15 connects well to the end of verse 5 of chapter 14. Here John sees the same assembly of overcomers: *". . . Them that had gotten the victory . . . they sing the song of Moses the servant of God and the song of the Lamb . . ."* This chapter is a victory celebration as seven angels are mandated to pour out the seven vials of the wrath of God.

A brief review: The Latter Church and the Jews have experienced seven years of opposition, persecution, and martyrdom; two three-and-one-half-year time frames. After the first three-and-one-half year Latter Rain ministry, the second season sees both Jew and Gentile fashioned, by fire, into God-sanctioned overcomers. It is the *"little season"* of Revelation 6:11. This period sees the martyrdom of the saints. This second three and one-half years, at its end, gives way to the eighth beast, having resident demonic presence, but yet an image of the seventh. So being, the ministry to the Gentiles has ceased, *"finished,"* and the Gentile judgment is determined. Thus, the statement *"filled up the wrath of God."* The Church is triumphant, *"They loved not their lives unto the death."* God is glorified and justified in the saints. They sing the song of Moses and the Lamb. All mankind should stand in awe, but they do not. Purging judgment awaits. Verse 4 above is a statement of pending vials: *"All nations shall come and worship before thee; for thy judgments are made manifest."*

VERSES 5–8: *5. "And after that I looked, and, behold, the temple of the tabernacle of the testimony in heaven was opened: 6. And the seven angels came out of the temple, having the seven plagues, clothed in pure and white linen, and having their breasts girded with golden girdles. 7. And one of the four beasts gave unto the seven angels seven golden vials full of the wrath of God, who liveth for ever and ever. 8. And the temple was filled with smoke from the glory of God, and from his power; and no man was able to enter into the temple, till the seven plagues of the seven angels were fulfilled."*

Earlier, John was told, *"Seal up those things which the seven thunders uttered, and write them not"* (Revelation 10:4). Now it is *"opened."* John reveals the *"things which the seven thunders uttered."* There would be no entry into the temple till the seven plagues were fulfilled, post-Armageddon and after the marriage supper of the Lamb.

Verse 7 above shows the seven angels are given seven golden vials full of the wrath of God. The seven angels are clothed in white linen and girded with golden girdles. If we can see the spiritual unity of this vision, it would include *"One like unto the Son of man . . . girt about the paps with a golden girdle"* (Revelation 1:13), and *"The souls of them that were slain for the word of God, and the testimony which they held . . . And white robes were given unto every one of them"* (Revelation 6:9, 11). We know that Jesus Christ and his elect are the first and then second witnesses that bear witness and judge. Jesus said, *"The testimony of two men is true"* (John 8:17). *"And Jesus said, For judgment I am come into this world, that they which see not might see; and that they which see might be made blind"* (John 9:39).

God's righteous judgment of the first heaven/first earth is going to be finished and the new heaven and new earth are going to be established. From the beginning, Jesus and his saints were ordained of God to accomplish his righteousness in the matter. That is our vision of things to come and our calling and purpose. We embrace the admonition, *"Stand therefore, having your loins girt about with truth, and having on the breastplate of righteousness"* (Ephesians 6:14). And, we believe the Scripture: *"And to her was granted that she should be arrayed in fine linen, clean and white: for the fine linen is the righteousness of saints"* (Revelation 19:8). In this life, justification is true only if we are 'in Christ.' *"For he hath made him to be sin for us, who knew no sin; that we might be made the righteousness of God in him"* (II Corinthians 5:21).

CHAPTER 16: *1. "And I heard a great voice out of the temple saying to the seven angels, Go your ways, and pour out the vials of the wrath of God upon the earth. 2. And the first went, and poured out his vial upon the earth; and there fell a noisome and grievous sore upon the men which had the mark of the beast, and upon them which worshipped his image. 3. And the second angel poured out his vial upon the sea; and it became as the blood of a dead man: and every living soul died in the sea. 4. And the third angel poured out his vial upon the rivers and fountains of waters; and they became blood. 5. And I heard the angel of the waters say, Thou art righteous, O Lord, which art, and wast, and shalt be, because thou hast judged thus. 6. For they have shed the blood of saints and prophets, and thou hast given them blood to drink; for they are worthy. 7. And I heard another out of the altar say, Even so, Lord God Almighty, true and righteous are thy judgments. 8. And the fourth angel poured out his vial upon the sun; and power was given unto him to scorch men with fire. 9. And men were scorched with great heat, and blasphemed the name of God, which hath power over these plagues: and they repented not to give him glory. 10. And the fifth angel poured out his vial upon the seat of the beast; and his kingdom was full of darkness; and they gnawed their tongues for pain, 11. And blasphemed the God of heaven because of their pains and their sores, and repented not of their deeds. 12. And the sixth angel poured out his vial upon the great river Euphrates; and the water thereof was dried up, that the way of the kings of the east might be prepared. 13. And I saw three unclean spirits like frogs come out of the mouth of the dragon, and out of the mouth of the beast, and out of the mouth of the false prophet. 14. For they are the spirits of devils, working miracles, which go forth unto the kings of the earth and of the whole world, to gather them to the battle of that great day of God Almighty. 15. Behold, I come as a thief. Blessed is he that watcheth, and keepeth his garments, lest he walk naked, and they see his shame. 16. And he gathered them together into a place called in the Hebrew tongue Armageddon. 17. And the seventh angel poured out his vial into the air; and there came a great voice out of the temple of heaven, from the throne, saying, It is done. 18. And there were voices, and thunders, and lightnings; and there was a great earthquake, such as was not since men were upon the earth, so mighty an earthquake, and so great. 19. And the great city was divided into three parts, and the cities of the nations fell: and great Babylon came in remembrance before God, to give unto her the cup of the wine of the fierceness of his wrath. 20. And every island fled away, and the mountains were not found. 21. And there fell upon men a great hail out of heaven, every stone about the weight of a talent: and men blasphemed God because of the plague of the hail; for the plague thereof was exceeding great."*

It is the beginning seven and one-half years of Christ's millennial reign; the time of the seventh seal, being seven thunders and seven vials. Again, mentioning the similitude: It is the 'Hebron' season of David's reign; the Lord's reign.

VERSES 1–9: *1. "And I heard a great voice out of the temple saying to the seven angels, Go your ways, and pour out the vials of the wrath of God upon the earth. 2. And the first went, and poured out his vial upon the earth; and there fell a noisome and grievous sore upon the men which had the mark of the beast, and upon them which worshipped his image. 3. And the second angel poured out his vial upon the sea; and it became as the blood of a dead man: and every living soul died in the sea. 4. And the third angel poured out his vial upon the rivers and fountains of waters; and they became blood. 5. And I heard the angel of the waters say, Thou art righteous, O Lord, which art, and wast, and shalt be, because thou hast judged thus. 6. For they have shed the blood of saints and prophets, and thou hast given them blood to drink; for they are worthy. 7. And I heard another out of the altar say, Even so, Lord God Almighty, true and righteous are thy judgments. 8. And the fourth angel poured out his vial upon the sun; and power was given unto him to scorch men with fire. 9. And men were scorched with great heat, and blasphemed the name of God, which hath power over these plagues: and they repented not to give him glory."*

Chapter 16 follows *"caught up,"* of Revelation 12:5. In chapters 14 and 15, they sing the song of Moses and the Lamb. Now, chapter 16 begins God's purging wrath of the up-front seven and one-half years of the millennium day of the Lord. Again, it is now the time of the opening of the seventh seal and the third woe and the thunderous outpouring of seven vials of the wrath of God into the earth.

A student of Revelation will see the similarity of the first four seals to this composite seven thunders/vials/plagues of the seventh angel/seventh seal. The distinction being: This seventh seal/third woe is a fullness, compared to the mitigated 'one-third' judgment of the first four seals. A study of the Zechariah text, chapters 13 and 14, leads us to think that this third woe is likely a 'two-thirds' destruction. Especially referring to the remanent Jew. *"And I will bring the third part through the fire, and will refine them as silver is refined, and will try them as gold is tried: they shall call on my name, and I will hear them: I will say, It is my people: and they shall say, The Lord is my God"* (Zechariah 13:9).

The vials are poured *"upon the earth . . . upon the sea . . . upon the rivers and fountains of waters"* and *"upon the sun."* Before the fall, man had dominion in three. And now, by God's providence and beyond the lost earth dominions, the fourth heavenly domain turns against him. That is to say: The vial poured out *"upon the sun"* is touching God's domain. This judgment causes mankind to *"blaspheme the name of God."* This world is judged.

VERSES 10–11: *10. "And the fifth angel poured out his vial upon the seat of the beast; and his kingdom was full of darkness; and they gnawed their tongues for pain, 11. And blasphemed the God of heaven because of their pains and their sores, and repented not of their deeds."*

It was stated earlier in the writing that there may be a break at the three-and-one-half-year mark. The break at verse 10 is indicative of that possibility.

Darkness and pain did not alter their total rebellion against God. Scripture states, *"For rebellion is as the sin of witchcraft, and stubbornness is as iniquity and idolatry"* (I Samuel 15:23). In Revelation 17:3, it is a woman that sits upon the scarlet-colored beast. She is a whorish false religious controlling power and unfaithful to the truth. She is 'witchcraft' and the 'man of sin' is the soul, the expression on earth, of the 'beast.' Typical of rebellion, the wicked *"blasphemed the God of heaven . . . and repented not of their deeds."*

VERSES 12–16: *12. "And the sixth angel poured out his vial upon the great river Euphrates; and the water thereof was dried up, that the way of the kings of the east might be prepared. 13. And I saw three unclean spirits like frogs come out of the mouth of the dragon, and out of the mouth of the beast, and out of the mouth of the false prophet. 14. For they are the spirits of devils, working miracles, which go forth unto the kings of the earth and of the whole world, to gather them to the battle of that great day of God Almighty. 15. Behold, I come as a thief. Blessed is he that watcheth, and keepeth his garments, lest he walk naked, and they see his shame. 16. And he gathered them together into a place called in the Hebrew tongue Armageddon."*

Earlier, in the time of the sixth seal opening, a voice from the four horns of the golden altar before God spoke; *"Loose the four angels which are bound in the great river Euphrates"* (Revelation 9:14). Thenceforward, *"the water thereof was dried up"* (verse 12). This is preparatory to the gathering together and the eventual 'event' of the Armageddon war. The *"dragon"* is the spirit-power, and his judgment is pending. The *"beast"* is the embodiment of the fallen estate of mankind. The *"false prophet"* reflects the mind, will, and emotion of this fallen estate. These three are likened in their expression to frogs. Basest of the base. God allows the working of miracles. It serves his purpose of gathering rebellious mankind unto judgment. These three reflect the spirit, body, and soul, respectively, of rebellion against God. Again, a six, six, six.

VERSES 17–21: *17. "And the seventh angel poured out his vial into the air; and there came a great voice out of the temple of heaven, from the throne, saying, It is done. 18. And there were voices, and thunders, and lightnings; and there was a great earthquake, such as was not since men were upon the earth, so mighty an earthquake, and so great. 19. And the great city was divided into three parts, and the cities of the nations fell: and great Babylon came in remembrance before God, to give unto her the cup of the wine of the fierceness of his wrath. 20. And every island fled away, and the mountains were not found. 21. And there fell upon men a great hail out of heaven, every stone about the weight of a talent: and men blasphemed God because of the plague of the hail; for the plague thereof was exceeding great."*

The seventh angel is the seventh of seven. This is the finality, and it is the judgment of what Paul termed *"the prince of the power of the air, the spirit that now worketh in the children of disobedience"* (Ephesians 2:2). The *"great voice"* saying *"it is done"* is God's just judgment upon the highest level of evil.

The world war ending Gentile times and the Armageddon war are connected. A great intellect said something to the effect: If there was another world war, it would be so devastating that the next war may be fought with sticks and stones. Consider the possibility: After a future, final world war, the Armageddon war may lack sophistication. The closing verses of this chapter show the destroying judgments of God being accomplished by natural phenomena more than by the instruments of man's war machine. None shall escape. So being, Babylon would be judged and any unity relating to the Abraham Accords is lost, Jew, Moslem, and Christian. The then-existent world of unbelief would be devoid of any willingness or hope of reconciliation. With the opposition against the Lord being judged, God and his Son, and his Body of Believers would be forevermore justified.

CHAPTER XIV

REVELATION, CHAPTERS 17-18

CHAPTER 17: *1. "And there came one of the seven angels which had the seven vials, and talked with me, saying unto me, Come hither; I will shew unto thee the judgment of the great whore that sitteth upon many waters: 2. With whom the kings of the earth have committed fornication, and the inhabitants of the earth have been made drunk with the wine of her fornication. 3. So he carried me away in the spirit into the wilderness: and I saw a woman sit upon a scarlet coloured beast, full of names of blasphemy, having seven heads and ten horns. 4. And the woman was arrayed in purple and scarlet colour, and decked with gold and precious stones and pearls, having a golden cup in her hand full of abominations and filthiness of her fornication: 5. And upon her forehead was a name written, MYSTERY, BABYLON THE GREAT, THE MOTHER OF HARLOTS AND ABOMINATIONS OF THE EARTH. 6. And I saw the woman drunken with the blood of the saints, and with the blood of the martyrs of Jesus: and when I saw her, I wondered with great admiration. 7. And the angel said unto me, Wherefore didst thou marvel? I will tell thee the mystery of the woman, and of the beast that carrieth her, which hath the seven heads and ten horns. 8. The beast that thou sawest was, and is not; and shall ascend out of the bottomless pit, and go into perdition: and they that dwell on the earth shall wonder, whose names were not written in the book of life from the foundation of the world, when they behold the beast that was, and is not, and yet is. 9. And here is the mind which hath wisdom. The seven heads are seven mountains, on which the woman sitteth. 10. And there are seven kings: five are fallen, and one is, and the other is not yet come; and when he cometh, he must continue a short space. 11. And the beast that was, and is not, even he is the eighth, and is of the seven, and goeth into perdition. 12. And the ten horns which thou sawest are ten kings, which have received no kingdom as yet; but receive power as kings one hour with the beast. 13. These have one mind, and shall give their power and strength unto the beast. 14. These shall make war with the Lamb, and the Lamb shall overcome them: for he is Lord of lords, and King of kings: and they that are with him are called, and chosen, and faithful. 15. And he saith unto me, The waters which thou sawest, where the whore sitteth, are peoples, and multitudes, and nations, and tongues. 16. And the ten horns which thou sawest upon the beast, these shall hate the whore, and shall make her desolate and naked, and shall eat her flesh, and burn her with fire. 17. For God hath put in their hearts to fulfil his will, and to agree, and give their kingdom unto the beast, until the words of God shall be fulfilled. 18. And the woman which thou sawest is that great city, which reigneth over the kings of the earth."*

John is shown the judgment of the false religious system. The evil empire is described in terms of its power, tenure, and downfall. The angel required John to deny awe or empathy toward this evil system.

Chapter 17 focuses on the concluding anti-Christ religious system and especially the eighth beast. John is being shown the judgment of the seventh and eighth beast. Again, the seventh beast and the eighth were inclusive of all. The eight beast is integrated with the dragon by virtue of mankind becoming demon-infested. More than varying degrees of demonic influence, many of mankind fall into 'possession' by disembodied spirits; that rank of demons who not only *"kept not their first estate, but left their own habitation . . ."* (Jude 6). Possibly a third of demons fallen-from-favor are not disembodied. Possibly two-thirds, dating from the time of the Flood, are disembodied spirits. Some fraction did find residence in human flesh, as evidenced in the New Testament. In the time of the eighth beast, that possession will be manifold. Repeating an earlier discussion: The opening of the *"bottomless pit,"* Revelation 9:1–2, will be that infestation of demons marking the beginning of the *"short time"* of the eighth beast. And, that is coincidental with the initiation of the *"judgment of the great day"* (Jude 6). Fallen humanity will be convinced of that. To wit: *". . . Woe to the inhabiters of the earth and of the sea! for the devil is come down unto you, having great wrath, because he knoweth that he hath but a short time"* (Revelation 12:12).

Chapter 17 treats the seventh beast and the eighth beast as a composite until verse 7. At that juncture, the angel begins to reveal the mystery of the judgment of the combined seventh and eighth heads of the beast. This judgment can be understood to be the judgment of heaven and earth. It is revelatory to understand that phenomenon. In that light, a student of the Revelation text may see the dragon as synonymous with civil powers. Given the correct timing, that is an accurate observation. That is, when civil powers fall into total unity with the dragon.

Chapter 17 shows us two prominent self-serving bodies. One: False religion. The false church, *". . . the great whore that setteth upon many waters."* A like-figure: *"For she sitteth at the door of her house, on a seat in the high places of the city, To call passengers who go right on their ways: Whoso is simple, let him turn in hither: and as for him that wanteth understanding, she saith to him, Stolen waters are sweet, and bread eaten in secret is pleasant. But he knoweth not that the dead are there; and that her guests are in the depths of hell"* (Proverbs 9:14–18). She is a religious system. Finally, she is possessed and infested with demons and committed to serving *"the prince of the power of the air, the spirit that now worketh in the children of disobedience"* (Ephesians 2:2). The 'voice,' soul/manifest psyche, of the false religious system is the false prophet. Likely, that person will be in unity with the prince of evil. 'Possessed' of the devil would be unity of a special description. Another like-figure: Jeremiah 5:30–31; *"A wonderful and horrible thing is committed in the land; The prophets prophesy falsely, and the priests bear rule by their means; and my people love to have it so: and what will ye do in the end thereof?"* So, fitting the carnal comfort zone, the greater the lie, the better the 'sell' to those blind of spiritual sight.

The other body: The civil powers or world powers, including kings, peoples, and nations; the 'beast.' The continuity factor is the continuing satanic inspiration. So being, it is historically inclusive and viewed as one beast with seven heads. This beast, by definition, is a dangerous wild, venomous creature; nightmarish to the unsuspecting.

The union of these two bodies, religious and civil, is *spiritual adultery*. It is a mix of iron and clay. There is a spirit of despising and accusation that flavors their convoluted togetherness. Eventually, there is blatant hatred. Prophetic statements by Daniel, as well as the Revelation text, show us there will be nakedness and burning in that divided camp. Scripture declares, *"And as the toes of the feet were part of iron, and part of clay, so the kingdom shall be partly strong, and partly broken. And whereas thou sawest iron mixed with miry clay, they shall mingle themselves with the seed of men: but they shall not cleave one to another, even as iron is not mixed with clay. And in the days of these kings shall the God of heaven set up a kingdom, which shall never be destroyed: and the kingdom shall not be left to other people, but it shall break in pieces and consume all these kingdoms, and it shall stand for ever"* (Daniel 2:42–44).

VERSES 1–2: *1. "And there came one of the seven angels which had the seven vials, and talked with me, saying unto me, Come hither; I will shew unto thee the judgment of the great whore that sitteth upon many waters: 2. With whom the kings of the earth have committed fornication, and the inhabitants of the earth have been made drunk with the wine of her fornication."*

John is to be shown the *"judgment of the great whore."* The time of judgment is the seventh seal/third woe, after the advent of the seventh and eighth heads. The judgment is justified at the *"finished,"* as it was with Christ on the cross. That is the vantage point from which John sees the vision. Before the angel reveals the judgment, he shows John the magnitude of the deception. Seven vials of the wrath of God are determined and John is prepared and instructed as to 'what is the mind of the Lord.' What he sees is the unmitigated judgment on the civil-religious combine. It was referred to in Daniel 2:31–45. Noted here are verses 33–35. *"His legs of iron, his feet part of iron and part of clay. Thou sawest till that a stone was cut out without hands, which smote the image upon his feet that were of iron and clay and brake them to pieces . . . and the stone that smote the image became a great mountain, and filled the whole earth."* Concerning that stone, God's ordained headship, as prophesied: *"And it shall come to pass in the last days, that the mountain of the Lord's house shall be established in the top of the mountains, and shall be exalted above the hills; and all nations shall flow unto it"* (Isaiah 2:2).

VERSES 3–7: *3. "So he carried me away in the spirit into the wilderness: and I saw a woman sit upon a scarlet coloured beast, full of names of blasphemy, having seven heads and ten horns. 4. And the woman was arrayed in purple and scarlet colour, and decked with gold and precious stones and pearls, having a golden cup in her hand full of abominations and filthiness of her fornication: 5. And upon her forehead was a name written, MYSTERY, BABYLON THE GREAT, THE MOTHER OF HARLOTS AND ABOMINATIONS OF THE EARTH. 6. And I saw the woman drunken with the blood of the saints, and with the blood of the martyrs of Jesus: and when I saw her, I wondered with great admiration. 7. And the angel said unto me, wherefore didst thou marvel? I will tell thee the mystery of the woman, and of the beast that carrieth her, which hath the seven heads and ten horns.*

John was not taken to a heavenly-place event. He was taken to the *"wilderness"* because this thing was happening in the wilderness. It was glorified with all the tapestry of *"Sodom and Egypt."* The vision was a depiction of the rider of the beast. Beyond the 'beast,' John was seeing the 'headship' of the beast. This passage is dealing with both the voice, 'soul,' of the false religious system and also with the 'body' of the system. At that point, John was impressed, *"I wondered with great admiration."* The angel took exception and said, *"Wherefore didst thou marvel? I will tell thee the mystery of the woman, and of the beast that carrieth her . . ."* One aspect of the saints having the father's name written in their forehead's is that they have *"the mind which hath wisdom."* They discern the mystery of iniquity and they know the end of the matter. Especially the religious system that has preeminence. The last verse quoted above, concerning the blood of the martyrs, reminds us that an overcomer's life and death is God's justification in the judgment of evil; first, the testimony of Jesus and, secondly, the saints' sacrifice. To wit: *9. "And when he had opened the fifth seal, I saw under the altar the souls of them that were slain for the word of God, and for the testimony which they held: 10. And they cried with a loud voice, saying, How long, O Lord, holy and true, dost thou not judge and avenge our blood on them that dwell on the earth? 11. And white robes were given unto every one of them; and it was said unto them, that they should rest yet for a little season, until their fellow servants also and their brethren, that should be killed as they were, should be fulfilled"* (Revelation 6:9–11).

The reference of it being *'fulfilled'* was accomplished during this *"little season,"* fifth seal/first woe, as 'finished' by the events of the sixth seal/second woe.

VERSES 8–11: *8. The beast that thou sawest was, and is not; and shall ascend out of the bottomless pit, and go into perdition: and they that dwell on the earth shall wonder, whose names were not written in the book of life from the foundation of the world, when they behold the beast that was, and is not, and yet is. 9. And here is the mind which hath wisdom. The seven heads are seven mountains, on which the woman sitteth. 10. And there are seven kings: five are fallen, and one is, and the other is not yet come; and when he cometh, he must continue a short space. 11. And the beast that was, and is not, even he is the eighth, and is of the seven, and goeth into perdition."*

John's admiration soon changes to awe and dread. The angel begins to enlighten John concerning the foul nature of the mystery of the woman. First, he describes the beast. The seven heads are a composite of seven kingdoms of errant humanity having a history of opposing God and oppressing God's people. Egypt, Assyria, Babylon, Persia, and Greece are the *"five are fallen."* Rome, the sixth, current to John's writing, is the *"one is."* The seventh, *"the other is not yet come,"* is religious Rome. *"Ten horns"* are integral to the composite beast. The reference to ten horns equates to the feet members, ten toes, of the beast image, per Daniel's vision. The vision is referring to the judgment and end of Gentile rule. Again, the similitude of the ten horns is the ten toes of the beast system. John is seeing the ending seventh and eighth beast. The angel speaks of a future beast. Religious Rome.

After Christ's death and going into the dark ages, Rome's former absolute rule was nonexistent. Jesus wounded the head of the beast. Genesis 3:15–16 prophesied that the seed of the woman, Jesus, would bruise the serpent's head and the serpent would bruise his, Jesus', heel. That was God's ruling with the death of Christ on the cross. That happened during secular Rome's absolute rule and the serpent, dragon power, Rome's spirit-realm power, was cast down as unjustified. A head wound. Later, Martin Luther pronounced that 'the just shall live by faith.' With that declaration of Scripture, and that being published, Papal Rome suffered a head wound. John is exhorted; the forces of Satan, united with civil-religious power, *"shall ascend out of the bottomless pit, and go into perdition."*

VERSES 12–15: *12. "And the ten horns which thou sawest are ten kings, which have received no kingdom as yet; but receive power as kings one hour with the beast. 13. These have one mind, and shall give their power and strength unto the beast. 14. These shall make war with the Lamb, and the Lamb shall overcome them: for he is Lord of lords, and King of kings: and they that are with him are called, and chosen, and faithful. 15. And he saith unto me, The waters which thou sawest, where the whore sitteth, are peoples, and multitudes, and nations, and tongues."*

The ten kings will come together in agreement because they jointly see religion as the cause of turmoil in their hemisphere. Satan inspires division. He is 'adversary' and he is 'accuser.' In the realm of spiritually blind mankind, Satan is *"the spirit that now worketh in the children of disobedience"* (Ephesians 2:2). After the season of peace and safety, and in the light of the impending world war, the nations will unite with and support Middle East regional powers; total collusion, and it is anti-Christ. God allows the suffering and martyrdom of the saints. The beast upon which false religion reigns is defined as *"peoples, and multitudes, and nations, and tongues."*

VERSES 16–18: *16. "And the ten horns which thou sawest upon the beast, these shall hate the whore, and shall make her desolate and naked, and shall eat her flesh, and burn her with fire. 17. For God hath put in their hearts to fulfil his will, and to agree, and give their kingdom unto the beast, until the words of God shall be fulfilled. 18. And the woman which thou sawest is that great city, which reigneth over the kings of the earth."*

Religious and civil are like iron and clay. They may stick together to rid themselves of a common enemy, but they are inherently opposed to one another. Familiarity breeds contempt. False religion will prove to be the problem. The Scripture well states the end of the matter. The *"great city,"* the seat of the beast, and the whore are a unity. That system will be made desolate, naked, be eaten, and her flesh burned. Jumping ahead: Later in Revelation the finality is declared. To wit: *"And the beast was taken, and with him the false prophet that wrought miracles before him, with which he deceived them that had received the mark of the beast, and them that worshipped his image. These both were cast alive into a lake of fire burning with brimstone"* (Revelation 19:20).

CHAPTER 18: *1. "And after these things I saw another angel come down from heaven, having great power; and the earth was lightened with his glory. 2. And he cried mightily with a strong voice, saying, Babylon the great is fallen, is fallen, and is become the habitation of devils, and the hold of every foul spirit, and a cage of every unclean and hateful bird. 3. For all nations have drunk of the wine of the wrath of her fornication, and the kings of the earth have committed fornication with her, and the merchants of the earth are waxed rich through the abundance of her delicacies. 4. And I heard another voice from heaven, saying, Come out of her, my people, that ye be not partakers of her sins, and that ye receive not of her plagues. 5. For her sins have reached unto heaven, and God hath remembered her iniquities. 6. Reward her even as she rewarded you, and double unto her double according to her works: in the cup which she hath filled fill to her double. 7. How much she hath glorified herself, and lived deliciously, so much torment and sorrow give her: for she saith in her heart, I sit a queen, and am no widow, and shall see no sorrow. 8. Therefore shall her plagues come in one day, death, and mourning, and famine; and she shall be utterly burned with fire: for strong is the Lord God who judgeth her. 9. And the kings of the earth, who have committed fornication and lived deliciously with her, shall bewail her, and lament for her, when they shall see the smoke of her burning, 10. Standing afar off for the fear of her torment, saying, Alas, alas, that great city Babylon, that mighty city! for in one hour is thy judgment come. 11. And the merchants of the earth shall weep and mourn over her; for no man buyeth their merchandise any more: 12. The merchandise of gold, and silver, and precious stones, and of pearls, and fine linen, and purple, and silk, and scarlet, and all thyine wood, and all manner vessels of ivory, and all manner vessels of most precious wood, and of brass, and iron, and marble, 13. And cinnamon, and odours, and ointments, and frankincense, and wine, and oil, and fine flour, and wheat, and beasts, and sheep, and horses, and chariots, and slaves, and souls of men. 14. And the fruits that thy soul lusted after are departed from thee, and all things which were dainty and goodly are departed from thee, and thou shalt find them no more at all. 15. The merchants of these things, which were made rich by her, shall stand afar off for the fear of her torment, weeping and wailing, 16. And saying, Alas, alas, that great city, that was clothed in fine linen, and purple, and scarlet, and decked with gold, and precious stones, and pearls! 17. For in one hour so great riches is come to nought. And every shipmaster, and all the company in ships, and sailors, and as many as trade by sea, stood afar off, 18. And cried when they saw the smoke of her burning, saying, What city is like unto this great city! 19. And they cast dust on their heads, and cried, weeping and wailing, saying, Alas, alas, that great city, wherein were made rich all that had ships in the sea by reason of her costliness! for in one hour is she made desolate. 20. Rejoice over her, thou heaven, and ye holy apostles and prophets; for God hath avenged you on her. 21. And a mighty angel took up a stone like a great millstone, and cast it into the sea, saying, Thus with violence shall that great city Babylon be thrown down, and shall be found no more at all. 22. And the voice of harpers, and musicians, and of pipers, and trumpeters, shall be heard no more at all in thee; and no craftsman, of whatsoever craft he be, shall be found any more in thee; and the sound of a millstone shall be heard no more at all in thee; 23. And the light of a candle shall shine no more at all in thee; and the voice of the bridegroom and of the bride shall be heard no more at all in thee: for thy merchants were the great men of the earth; for by thy sorceries were all nations deceived. 24. And in her was found the blood of prophets, and of saints, and of all that were slain upon the earth."*

Babylon the great has fallen. The degree of corruption, her involvement and degradation of nations, is declared. Her power is diminished, and her tenure is ended. The previous chapter 17 focused on *"the judgment of the great whore that sitteth upon many waters."* And, the many waters here is the seventh transitioning into the eighth beast: *"The waters which thou sawest, where the whore sitteth, are peoples, and multitudes, and nations, and tongues."*

Chapter 18 focuses on the beast. The beast is Babylon and John hears the declaration of their estate: *"Babylon the great is fallen, is fallen, and is become the habitation of devils, and the hold of every foul spirit, and a cage of every unclean and hateful bird.* Furthermore, John *"heard another voice from heaven, saying, Come out of her, my people, that ye be not partakers of her sins, and that ye receive not of her plagues."*

Earlier in the Revelation, an event pertaining to 'circumstance' was recorded: *"And there was war in heaven: Michael and his angels fought against the dragon; and the dragon fought and his angels, And prevailed not; neither was their place found any more in heaven. And the great dragon was cast out, that old serpent, called the Devil, and Satan, which deceiveth the whole world: he was cast out into the earth, and his angels were cast out with him"* (Revelation 12:7–9). This Scripture pertained to the war of accusation against the saints and their justification against the saints. And, remember, this testimony of the saints is the second witness that judges, with righteous justification. It was the *"little season,"* time of martyrdom. The setting of this eighteenth chapter is validated because of this fact. It is God's righteousness and justification in this final judgment of the beast system. The forces of our righteous Lord were declared righteous, and they are victorious. The dragon, the old serpent, called the Devil and Satan lost their spirit habitation. Jude, verse 6 reads, *"kept not their first estate, but left their own habitation."* Please note: We do understand that Jude may have been referring explicitly to the judgment in Noah's time, but the *"unto the judgment of the great day"* was the part that pertained to this present Revelation setting. Babylon became demon-infested and gravitated from the seventh beast to the eighth beast. And, eight is the number of 'judgment.' This is the setting and basis for what is spoken in this eighteenth chapter.

The timing moves quickly to the seventh seal/third woe as per *"The second woe is past; and, behold, the third woe cometh quickly"* (Revelation 11:14).

VERSES 1–3: *1. "And after these things I saw another angel come down from heaven, having great power; and the earth was lightened with his glory. 2. And he cried mightily with a strong voice, saying, Babylon the great is fallen, is fallen, and is become the habitation of devils, and the hold of every foul spirit, and a cage of every unclean and hateful bird. 3. For all nations have drunk of the wine of the wrath of her fornication, and the kings of the earth have committed fornication with her, and the merchants of the earth are waxed rich through the abundance of her delicacies."*

The angel first mentioned having *"great power"* is reminiscent of the mighty angel of the Old Testament record. That is Michael. Daniel referred to him as the *"great prince."* Revelation 12:7 refers to Michael: *"And there was war in heaven: Michael and his angels fought against the dragon; and the dragon fought and his angels . . ."* It is reasonable that the archangel Michael, as an immediate emissary of God, is present. And, the other archangel, Gabriel, would be present. And, it would be his function to address the welfare of the saints. The text plainly declares the fallen estate of Babylon. Babylon equates to the beast as being the earthly headship of the beast; geographical and political. Looking at 'evil' as 'embodied,' the beast is the 'body,' and Babylon is the earthly component that sustains the false prophet.

VERSES 4–8: *4. "And I heard another voice from heaven, saying, Come out of her, my people, that ye be not partakers of her sins, and that ye receive not of her plagues. 5. For her sins have reached unto heaven, and God hath remembered her iniquities. 6. Reward her even as she rewarded you, and double unto her double according to her works: in the cup which she hath filled fill to her double. 7. How much she hath glorified herself, and lived deliciously, so much torment and sorrow give her: for she saith in her heart, I sit a queen, and am no widow, and shall see no sorrow. 8. Therefore shall her plagues come in one day, death, and mourning, and famine; and she shall be utterly burned with fire: for strong is the Lord God who judgeth her."*

The *"another voice from heaven,"* possibly Gabriel, addresses *"my people."* The people of God were exhorted to *"come out"* in the light of the horrific pending judgment of Babylon. Again, the exhortations were declared to John and certainly were directed at his generation, but we of this latter time are the citizens at greater risk. The text, as read, is a clarion call to stay clear of Babylonish entrapments. As stated by the last verse above, the judgments are without hesitation and decisive.

VERSES 9–13: *9. "And the kings of the earth, who have committed fornication and lived deliciously with her, shall bewail her, and lament for her, when they shall see the smoke of her burning, 10. Standing afar off for the fear of her torment, saying, Alas, alas, that great city Babylon, that mighty city! for in one hour is thy judgment come. 11. And the merchants of the earth shall weep and mourn over her; for no man buyeth their merchandise any more: 12. The merchandise of gold, and silver, and precious stones, and of pearls, and fine linen, and purple, and silk, and scarlet, and all thyine wood, and all manner vessels of ivory, and all manner vessels of most precious wood, and of brass, and iron, and marble, 13. And cinnamon, and odours, and ointments, and frankincense, and wine, and oil, and fine flour, and wheat, and beasts, and sheep, and horses, and chariots, and slaves, and souls of men."*

Ten kings were cohorts and parties to Babylon's demise. As stated in the previous chapter: *"And the ten horns which thou sawest upon the beast, these shall hate the whore, and shall make her desolate and naked, and shall eat her flesh, and burn her with fire. 17. For God hath put in their hearts to fulfil his will, and to agree, and give their kingdom unto the beast, until the words of God shall be fulfilled"* (Revelation 17:16). That *"until"* was allotted for God's purpose to complete the justification of the outpouring of God's wrath. Note: The *"kings of the earth"* mentioned in this eighteenth chapter likely includes greater than ten. The sundry *"merchandise"* indicates world trade. The mention of *"souls of men"* is indicative of the ungodly depraved nature of world affairs.

VERSES 14–19: *14. "And the fruits that thy soul lusted after are departed from thee, and all things which were dainty and goodly are departed from thee, and thou shalt find them no more at all. 15. The merchants of these things, which were made rich by her, shall stand afar off for the fear of her torment, weeping and wailing, 16. And saying, Alas, alas, that great city, that was clothed in fine linen, and purple, and scarlet, and decked with gold, and precious stones, and pearls! 17. "For in one hour so great riches is come to nought. And every shipmaster, and all the company in ships, and sailors, and as many as trade by sea, stood afar off, 18. And cried when they saw the smoke of her burning, saying, What city is like unto this great city! 19. And they cast dust on their heads, and cried, weeping and wailing, saying, Alas, alas, that great city, wherein were made rich all that had ships in the sea by reason of her costliness! for in one hour is she made desolate."*

The taking away of their rewards tell us that Babylon is lust-driven: lust of the flesh, lust of the eye, and the pride of life. The *"merchants of these things"* bemoaned Babylon's loss. This *"Alas, alas"* indicates the audience was a complicit world including the Middle East region and beyond. Further depiction and a second *"Alas, alas"* is declared with a time-mention of *"one hour."* The time-mention is with respect to swift judgment and connects with Revelation 11:13–14. To wit: *"And the same hour was there a great earthquake, and the tenth part of the city fell, and in the earthquake were slain of men seven thousand: and the remnant were affrighted, and gave glory to the God of heaven. 14. The second woe is past; and, behold, the third woe cometh quickly."*

VERSES 20–21: *20. "Rejoice over her, thou heaven, and ye holy apostles and prophets; for God hath avenged you on her. 21. And a mighty angel took up a stone like a great millstone, and cast it into the sea, saying, Thus with violence shall that great city Babylon be thrown down, and shall be found no more at all."*

There is no flavor of mercy or compassion toward Babylon. God has 'spoken' and only rejoicing is in order. The *"mighty angel"* is again acting on God's will and determinations. *"A great millstone"* implies overwhelming hardship; that was the current happening. *"And I beheld when he had opened the sixth seal, and, lo, there was a great earthquake; and the sun became black as sackcloth of hair, and the moon became as blood; And the stars of heaven fell unto the earth, even as a fig tree casteth her untimely figs, when she is shaken of a mighty wind. And the heaven departed as a scroll when it is rolled together; and every mountain and island were moved out of their places. And the kings of the earth, and the great men, and the rich men, and the chief captains, and the mighty men, and every bondman, and every free man, hid themselves in the dens and in the rocks of the mountains; And said to the mountains and rocks, Fall on us, and hide us from the face of him that sitteth on the throne, and from the wrath of the Lamb: For the great day of his wrath is come; and who shall be able to stand?"* (Revelation 6:12–17).

VERSES 22–24: *22. "And the voice of harpers, and musicians, and of pipers, and trumpeters, shall be heard no more at all in thee; and no craftsman, of whatsoever craft he be, shall be found any more in thee; and the sound of a millstone shall be heard no more at all in thee; 23. And the light of a candle shall shine no more at all in thee; and the voice of the bridegroom and of the bride shall be heard no more at all in thee: for thy merchants were the great men of the earth; for by thy sorceries were all nations deceived. 24. And in her was found the blood of prophets, and of saints, and of all that were slain upon the earth."*

All rejoicing in Babylon, both in man's affairs and rejoicing in spiritual matters, have ceased. Both have fallen away. In Old Testament terminology, Ichabod is written over the door. There is no glory to God, only *"fire burning with brimstone."*

Repeating: Befitting that time: *"And the same hour was there a great earthquake, and the tenth part of the city fell, and in the earthquake were slain of men seven thousand: and the remnant were affrighted, and gave glory to the God of heaven. 14. The second woe is past; and, behold, the third woe cometh quickly"* (Revelation 11:13–14).

CHAPTER XV

REVELATION, CHAPTER 19

CHAPTER 19: *1. "And after these things I heard a great voice of much people in heaven, saying, Alleluia; Salvation, and glory, and honour, and power, unto the Lord our God: 2. For true and righteous are his judgments: for he hath judged the great whore, which did corrupt the earth with her fornication, and hath avenged the blood of his servants at her hand. 3. And again they said, Alleluia. And her smoke rose up for ever and ever. 4. And the four and twenty elders and the four beasts fell down and worshipped God that sat on the throne, saying, Amen; Alleluia. 5. And a voice came out of the throne, saying, Praise our God, all ye his servants, and ye that fear him, both small and great. 6. And I heard as it were the voice of a great multitude, and as the voice of many waters, and as the voice of mighty thunderings, saying, Alleluia: for the Lord God omnipotent reigneth. 7. Let us be glad and rejoice, and give honour to him: for the marriage of the Lamb is come, and his wife hath made herself ready. 8. And to her was granted that she should be arrayed in fine linen, clean and white: for the fine linen is the righteousness of saints. 9. And he saith unto me, Write, Blessed are they which are called unto the marriage supper of the Lamb. And he saith unto me, These are the true sayings of God. 10. And I fell at his feet to worship him. And he said unto me, See thou do it not: I am thy fellowservant, and of thy brethren that have the testimony of Jesus: worship God: for the testimony of Jesus is the spirit of prophecy. 11. And I saw heaven opened, and behold a white horse; and he that sat upon him was called Faithful and True, and in righteousness he doth judge and make war. 12. His eyes were as a flame of fire, and on his head were many crowns; and he had a name written, that no man knew, but he himself. 13. And he was clothed with a vesture dipped in blood: and his name is called The Word of God. 14. And the armies which were in heaven followed him upon white horses, clothed in fine linen, white and clean. 15. And out of his mouth goeth a sharp sword, that with it he should smite the nations: and he shall rule them with a rod of iron: and he treadeth the winepress of the fierceness and wrath of Almighty God. 16. And he hath on his vesture and on his thigh a name written, KING OF KINGS, AND LORD OF LORDS. 17. And I saw an angel standing in the sun; and he cried with a loud voice, saying to all the fowls that fly in the midst of heaven, Come and gather yourselves together unto the supper of the great God; 18. That ye may eat the flesh of kings, and the flesh of captains, and the flesh of mighty men, and the flesh of horses, and of them that sit on them, and the flesh of all men, both free and bond, both small and great. 19. And I saw the beast, and the kings of the earth, and their armies, gathered together to make war against him that sat on the horse, and against his army. 20. And the beast was taken, and with him the false prophet that wrought miracles before him, with which he deceived them that had received the mark of the beast, and them that worshipped his image. These both were cast alive into a lake of fire burning with brimstone. 21. And the remnant were slain with the sword of him that sat upon the horse, which sword proceeded out of his mouth: and all the fowls were filled with their flesh."*

The setting is after the judgment of the great whore; *"for he hath judged the great whore."* It is now the time of retribution, *"For the Lord God omnipotent reigneth . . . for the marriage of the Lamb is come."* Chapter 19 proceeds to take us through the time of Armageddon to the 'event' of the Armageddon war and the final, concluding judgment. To wit: *"And the beast was taken, and with him the false prophet that wrought miracles before him, with which he deceived them that had received the mark of the beast, and them that worshipped his image. These both were cast alive into a lake of fire burning with brimstone."*

VERSES 1–3: *1. "And after these things I heard a great voice of much people in heaven, saying, Alleluia; Salvation, and glory, and honour, and power, unto the Lord our God: 2. For true and righteous are his judgments: for he hath judged the great whore, which did corrupt the earth with her fornication, and hath avenged the blood of his servants at her hand. 3. And again they said, Alleluia. And her smoke rose up for ever and ever."*

God's righteousness is demonstrated by the life and death of Christ, the first witness, and then the life and death of the saints, the second witness. The false religious system is judged. The spirit of the operation, headed in the spirit realm by Satan, is judged unworthy of a favored estate, and unworthy of his celestial habitation. Earlier, chapter 17 revealed the destruction of the whore at the hands of the ten kings who turned on her. *"And the ten horns which thou sawest upon the beast, these shall hate the whore, and shall make her desolate and naked, and shall eat her flesh, and burn her with fire."* Man's wrath, however destructive, in the finality, is secondary to God's judgment.

VERSES 4–6: *4. "And the four and twenty elders and the four beasts fell down and worshipped God that sat on the throne, saying, Amen; Alleluia. 5. And a voice came out of the throne, saying, Praise our God, all ye his servants, and ye that fear him, both small and great. 6. And I heard as it were the voice of a great multitude, and as the voice of many waters, and as the voice of mighty thunderings, saying, Alleluia: for the Lord God omnipotent reigneth."*

Heaven rejoices and we stand in awe to read the report. It is the same as chapter 14: *"And I looked, and, lo, a Lamb stood on the mount Sion, and with him an hundred forty and four thousand, having his Father's name written in their foreheads. 2. And I heard a voice from heaven, as the voice of many waters, and as the voice of a great thunder: and I heard the voice of harpers harping with their harps: 3. And they sung as it were a new song before the throne, and before the four beasts, and the elders: and no man could learn that song but the hundred and forty and four thousand, which were redeemed from the earth"* (Revelation 14:1–3).

VERSES 7–9: *7. "Let us be glad and rejoice, and give honour to him: for the marriage of the Lamb is come, and his wife hath made herself ready. 8. And to her was granted that she should be arrayed in fine linen, clean and white: for the fine linen is the righteousness of saints. 9. And he saith unto me, Write, Blessed are they which are called unto the marriage supper of the Lamb. And he saith unto me, These are the true sayings of God."*

These verses are to the glory of God. Again, we stand in awe just reading the report. It is the marriage supper of the Lamb, when the *"man child"* graduates to become *"his wife."*

The Lord's Day has come. Revelation 8:1, *"When he had opened the seventh seal there was silence in heaven about the space of half an hour."* It is the opening seven and one-half years of Christ's one thousand years millennium reign. The in-earth happening is the third woe. A time of seven thunders declaring seven vials of the wrath of God, and those plagues poured into the earth. A time of wars and rumors of wars. The time of gathering unto the event of the Armageddon war.

VERSE 10: *"And I fell at his feet to worship him. And he said unto me, See thou do it not: I am thy fellowservant, and of thy brethren that have the testimony of Jesus: worship God: for the testimony of Jesus is the spirit of prophecy."*

This *"fellowservant"* who refused worship is thought to be the prophet Daniel. As discussed earlier, this writer connects him with *"his angel"* mentioned in the first verse of Revelation. In this instance, we are given the impression of an 'interface' with Jesus. The statement *"the testimony of Jesus is the spirit of prophecy"* is to the glory of God. Jesus is the *"Alpha and Omega, the first and the last."* Being obedient, Jesus fulfilled all prophecy to the glory of the Father. In a profoundly glorious way, Jesus, Daniel, and John are one gold in God.

VERSES 11–16: *11. "And I saw heaven opened, and behold a white horse; and he that sat upon him was called Faithful and True, and in righteousness he doth judge and make war. 12. His eyes were as a flame of fire, and on his head were many crowns; and he had a name written, that no man knew, but he himself. 13. And he was clothed with a vesture dipped in blood: and his name is called The Word of God. 14. And the armies which were in heaven followed him upon white horses, clothed in fine linen, white and clean. 15. And out of his mouth goeth a sharp sword, that with it he should smite the nations: and he shall rule them with a rod of iron: and he treadeth the winepress of the fierceness and wrath of Almighty God. 16. And he hath on his vesture and on his thigh a name written, KING OF KINGS, AND LORD OF LORDS."*

The revelation of Jesus in these verses declares his glorious attributes and titles. *"Which in his times he shall shew, who is the blessed and only Potentate, the King of kings, and Lord of lords"* (I Timothy 6:15). Jesus is also the rider of the white horse mentioned earlier; *"And I saw, and behold a white horse: and he that sat on him had a bow; and a crown was given unto him: and he went forth conquering, and to conquer"* (Revelation 6:2).

VERSES 17–19: *17. "And I saw an angel standing in the sun; and he cried with a loud voice, saying to all the fowls that fly in the midst of heaven, Come and gather yourselves together unto the supper of the great God; 18. That ye may eat the flesh of kings, and the flesh of captains, and the flesh of mighty men, and the flesh of horses, and of them that sit on them, and the flesh of all men, both free and bond, both small and great. 19. And I saw the beast, and the kings of the earth, and their armies, gathered together to make war against him that sat on the horse, and against his army."*

This *"supper of the great God"* is going to be the glorious revelation of God's judgment on the beast and the false prophet. Ezekiel prophesied this event with like-vision, like-detail. *"And, thou son of man, thus saith the Lord God; Speak unto every feathered fowl, and to every beast of the field, Assemble yourselves, and come; gather yourselves on every side to my sacrifice that I do sacrifice for you, even a great sacrifice upon the mountains of Israel, that ye may eat flesh, and drink blood"* (Ezekiel 39:17). The chapter, in total, supports the vision of the final Armageddon judgment. The time and setting are the same *"marriage supper of the Lamb"* (Revelation 19:9).

VERSES 20–21: *20. "And the beast was taken, and with him the false prophet that wrought miracles before him, with which he deceived them that had received the mark of the beast, and them that worshipped his image. These both were cast alive into a lake of fire burning with brimstone. 21. And the remnant were slain with the sword of him that sat upon the horse, which sword proceeded out of his mouth: and all the fowls were filled with their flesh."*

Of all that is spoken in Scripture, and all comments, this is the concluding earthly judgment. That is, the soul or psyche, and body or embodiment, of evil on earth is judged, and what remained was food for the fowls.

CHAPTER XVI

REVELATION, CHAPTER 20

CHAPTER 20: *1. "And I saw an angel come down from heaven, having the key of the bottomless pit and a great chain in his hand. 2. And he laid hold on the dragon, that old serpent, which is the Devil, and Satan, and bound him a thousand years, 3. And cast him into the bottomless pit, and shut him up, and set a seal upon him, that he should deceive the nations no more, till the thousand years should be fulfilled: and after that he must be loosed a little season. 4. And I saw thrones, and they sat upon them, and judgment was given unto them: and I saw the souls of them that were beheaded for the witness of Jesus, and for the word of God, and which had not worshipped the beast, neither his image, neither had received his mark upon their foreheads, or in their hands; and they lived and reigned with Christ a thousand years. 5. But the rest of the dead lived not again until the thousand years were finished. This is the first resurrection. 6. Blessed and holy is he that hath part in the first resurrection: on such the second death hath no power, but they shall be priests of God and of Christ, and shall reign with him a thousand years. 7. And when the thousand years are expired, Satan shall be loosed out of his prison, 8. And shall go out to deceive the nations which are in the four quarters of the earth, Gog and Magog, to gather them together to battle: the number of whom is as the sand of the sea. 9. And they went up on the breadth of the earth, and compassed the camp of the saints about, and the beloved city: and fire came down from God out of heaven, and devoured them. 10. And the devil that deceived them was cast into the lake of fire and brimstone, where the beast and the false prophet are, and shall be tormented day and night for ever and ever. 11. And I saw a great white throne, and him that sat on it, from whose face the earth and the heaven fled away; and there was found no place for them. 12. And I saw the dead, small and great, stand before God; and the books were opened: and another book was opened, which is the book of life: and the dead were judged out of those things which were written in the books, according to their works. 13. And the sea gave up the dead which were in it; and death and hell delivered up the dead which were in them: and they were judged every man according to their works. 14. And death and hell were cast into the lake of fire. This is the second death. 15. And whosoever was not found written in the book of life was cast into the lake of fire."*

This chapter begins with the Devil being bound for a thousand years. It is seven and one-half years into Christ's millennium reign. The beast and the false prophet are already judged and sentenced. See Revelation 19:20. Chapter 20 ends one thousand years later with the judgment and sentencing of the devil and all who are contrary to God.

VERSES 1–3: *1. "And I saw an angel come down from heaven, having the key of the bottomless pit and a great chain in his hand. 2. And he laid hold on the dragon, that old serpent, which is the Devil, and Satan, and bound him a thousand years, 3. And cast him into the bottomless pit, and shut him up, and set a seal upon him, that he should deceive the nations no more, till the thousand years should be fulfilled: and after that he must be loosed a little season."*

The dispatch of the *"angel come down from heaven,"* and his cause, reflects God's righteousness, his glory, and his power. The devil is bound and cast into the bottomless pit. The *"great chain"* has been compared to the justified lives of believers who *"loved not their lives unto the death."* The devil's role as deceiver is clearly stated. The *"bottomless pit"* is a place without foundation. Jesus told his disciples, *"Upon this rock I will build my church; and the gates of hell shall not prevail against it"* (Matthew 16:18). Anything not built on Christ is foundationless.

This ending comment of verse 3, *"and after that he must be loosed a little season,"* is a jumping-ahead statement. That is, at the end of the thousand years, the devil will be loosed a little season. The term *'little season'* has been treated as three and one-half years. That jumping-ahead statement is refreshed in verse 7.

VERSE 4: *"And I saw thrones, and they sat upon them, and judgment was given unto them: and I saw the souls of them that were beheaded for the witness of Jesus, and for the word of God, and which had not worshipped the beast, neither his image, neither had received his mark upon their foreheads, or in their hands; and they lived and reigned with Christ a thousand years."*

John saw the victorious bride of Christ in their God-given rightful place of judgment with Jesus Christ. *"To him that overcometh will I grant to sit with me in my throne, even as I also overcame, and am set down with my Father in his throne"* (Revelation 3:21). They sat upon thrones judging during the thousand years millennium reign of Christ.

VERSES 5–6: *5. "But the rest of the dead lived not again until the thousand years were finished. This is the first resurrection. 6. Blessed and holy is he that hath part in the first resurrection: on such the second death hath no power, but they shall be priests of God and of Christ, and shall reign with him a thousand years."*

The second sentence of verse 5, *"This is the first resurrection,"* connects to the overcomers of verse 4. They are the bride. They are the first resurrection souls. These are the 144,000 who are *"caught up unto God, and to his throne."* They are granted immortality and celestial habitation.

The first mention of the fifth verse, *"But the rest of the dead lived not again until the thousand years were finished,"* is after the millennium. The *"rest of the dead"* refers to the saints that have died worthy of a resurrection. Other than the first resurrection saints, no person would resurrect unto eternal life until the final resurrection.

VERSES 7–10: *7. "And when the thousand years are expired, Satan shall be loosed out of his prison, 8. And shall go out to deceive the nations which are in the four quarters of the earth, Gog and Magog, to gather them together to battle: the number of whom is as the sand of the sea. 9. And they went up on the breadth of the earth, and compassed the camp of the saints about, and the beloved city: and fire came down from God out of heaven, and devoured them. 10. And the devil that deceived them was cast into the lake of fire and brimstone, where the beast and the false prophet are, and shall be tormented day and night for ever and ever."*

Satan has been bound for a thousand years. In the earth, there lacked continuity with the beast historical headships. Satan was that spirit unity. Now he continues his work of enmity against God and God's people. His audience is myriad; the latter-time Gog and Magog. He gathers adherents worldwide to overtake God's saints and beloved city. There is no battle of Gog and Magog. It is not a battle. God totally devoured them by fire and cast the devil into the lake of fire. The like-event happened to the beast and the false prophet one thousand years earlier.

VERSES 11–13: *11. "And I saw a great white throne, and him that sat on it, from whose face the earth and the heaven fled away; and there was found no place for them. 12. And I saw the dead, small and great, stand before God; and the books were opened: and another book was opened, which is the book of life: and the dead were judged out of those things which were written in the books, according to their works. 13. And the sea gave up the dead which were in it; and death and hell delivered up the dead which were in them: and they were judged every man according to their works."*

It is now the time of the *"great white throne."* The terminology *"the earth and the heaven fled away"* bears a similarity to Paul's referencing the Psalms: *"And, Thou, Lord, in the beginning hast laid the foundation of the earth; and the heavens are the works of thine hands: They shall perish; but thou remainest; and they all shall wax old as doth a garment; And as a vesture shalt thou fold them up, and they shall be changed; but thou art the same, and thy years shall not fail"* (Hebrews 1:10–12).

"The dead, small and great, stand before God." To these *"the book of life"* was opened and they were judged *"according to their works."* These are in *"the book of life."* This portends a good estate. The following did not *"stand before God."* That is, those in *"the sea"* and those in *"death and hell."* The Psalmist stated, *"Therefore the ungodly shall not stand in the judgment, not sinners in the congregation of the righteous. For the Lord knoweth the way of the righteous: but the way of the ungodly shall perish"* (Psalms 1:5–6). The *"sea"* is the untold millions of mankind that know not God. Those in *"death and hell"* are those knowing God and yet are unworthy of a resurrection unto life. It is likely neither of the latter two groups reappeared as individualities. More likely their hopeless 'estate' was addressed. As the Psalmist stated, *"The way* (estate) *of the ungodly shall perish."*

VERSES 14–15: *14. "And death and hell were cast into the lake of fire. This is the second death. 15. And whosoever was not found written in the book of life was cast into the lake of fire."*

In a final sense, *"death and hell"* equates to *"the first heaven and the first earth."* Both exist because of and are under the auspices of Satan. Both evil parties, things in heaven and things on earth, are relegated to *"the lake of fire. This is the second death."*

CHAPTER XVII

REVELATION, CHAPTERS 21-22

CHAPTER 21: *1. "And I saw a new heaven and a new earth: for the first heaven and the first earth were passed away; and there was no more sea. 2. And I John saw the holy city, new Jerusalem, coming down from God out of heaven, prepared as a bride adorned for her husband. 3. And I heard a great voice out of heaven saying, Behold, the tabernacle of God is with men, and he will dwell with them, and they shall be his people, and God himself shall be with them, and be their God. 4. And God shall wipe away all tears from their eyes; and there shall be no more death, neither sorrow, nor crying, neither shall there be any more pain: for the former things are passed away. 5. And he that sat upon the throne said, Behold, I make all things new. And he said unto me, Write: for these words are true and faithful. 6. And he said unto me, It is done. I am Alpha and Omega, the beginning and the end. I will give unto him that is athirst of the fountain of the water of life freely. 7. He that overcometh shall inherit all things; and I will be his God, and he shall be my son. 8. But the fearful, and unbelieving, and the abominable, and murderers, and whoremongers, and sorcerers, and idolaters, and all liars, shall have their part in the lake which burneth with fire and brimstone: which is the second death. 9. And there came unto me one of the seven angels which had the seven vials full of the seven last plagues, and talked with me, saying, Come hither, I will shew thee the bride, the Lamb's wife. 10. And he carried me away in the spirit to a great and high mountain, and shewed me that great city, the holy Jerusalem, descending out of heaven from God, 11. Having the glory of God: and her light was like unto a stone most precious, even like a jasper stone, clear as crystal; 12. And had a wall great and high, and had twelve gates, and at the gates twelve angels, and names written thereon, which are the names of the twelve tribes of the children of Israel: 13. On the east three gates; on the north three gates; on the south three gates; and on the west three gates. 14. And the wall of the city had twelve foundations, and in them the names of the twelve apostles of the Lamb. 15. And he that talked with me had a golden reed to measure the city, and the gates thereof, and the wall thereof. 16. And the city lieth foursquare, and the length is as large as the breadth: and he measured the city with the reed, twelve thousand furlongs. The length and the breadth and the height of it are equal. 17. And he measured the wall thereof, an hundred and forty and four cubits, according to the measure of a man, that is, of the angel. 18. And the building of the wall of it was of jasper: and the city was pure gold, like unto clear glass. 19. And the foundations of the wall of the city were garnished with all manner of precious stones. The first foundation was jasper; the second, sapphire; the third, a chalcedony; the fourth, an emerald; 20. The fifth, sardonyx; the sixth, sardius; the seventh, chrysolite; the eighth, beryl; the ninth, a topaz; the tenth, a chrysoprasus; the eleventh, a jacinth; the twelfth, an amethyst. 21. And the twelve gates were twelve pearls; every several gate was of one pearl: and the street of the city was pure gold, as it were transparent glass. 22. And I saw no temple therein: for the Lord God Almighty and the Lamb are the temple of it. 23. And the city had no need of the sun, neither of the moon, to shine in it: for the glory of God did lighten it, and the Lamb is the light thereof. 24. And the nations of them which are saved shall walk in the light of it: and the kings of the earth do bring their glory and honour into it. 25. And the gates of it shall not be shut at all by day: for there shall be no night there. 26. And they shall bring the glory and honour of the nations into it. 27. And there shall in no wise enter into it any thing that defileth, neither whatsoever worketh abomination, or maketh a lie: but they which are written in the Lamb's book of life."*

The focus is the holy city, new Jerusalem. The final judgment has been accomplished. All things contrary to God are 'perished.' The first Adam failed in keeping the garden of God. Jesus, the second Adam, did not fail. Chapter 21 clearly and wonderfully describes *"a new heaven and a new earth."*

VERSES 1–3: *1. "And I saw a new heaven and a new earth: for the first heaven and the first earth were passed away; and there was no more sea. 2. And I John saw the holy city, new Jerusalem, coming down from God out of heaven, prepared as a bride adorned for her husband. 3. And I heard a great voice out of heaven saying, Behold, the tabernacle of God is with men, and he will dwell with them, and they shall be his people, and God himself shall be with them, and be their God."*

The citizens of this final blessed estate are both terrestrial mortals having eternal life, and celestial immortals having immortality. The bride of Christ occupies new Jerusalem. All similitudes are 'finished.' The gates and veils are *"done away."* And, Christ's work has fully accomplished God the Father's *"Word,"* his plan, and his intent. *"For he is our peace, who hath made both one, and hath broken down the middle wall of partition between us; Having abolished in his flesh the enmity, even the law of commandments contained in ordinances; for to make in himself of twain one new man, so making peace"* (Ephesians 2:14–15). This Scripture touches not just the cessation of the enmity between Jew and Gentile, but more perfectly, the ceasing of enmity between God and man. The shadow on earth of heavenly things becomes a present reality and there is no need for similitudes. To wit: *"The tabernacle of God is with men."*

Relating to the statement *"no more sea,"* Paul writes, *"And they shall not teach every man his neighbour, and every man his brother, saying, Know the Lord: for all shall know me, from the least to the greatest"* (Hebrews 8:11).

VERSES 4–8: *4. And God shall wipe away all tears from their eyes; and there shall be no more death, neither sorrow, nor crying, neither shall there be any more pain: for the former things are passed away. 5. And he that sat upon the throne said, Behold, I make all things new. And he said unto me, Write: for these words are true and faithful. 6. And he said unto me, It is done. I am Alpha and Omega, the beginning and the end. I will give unto him that is athirst of the fountain of the water of life freely. 7. He that overcometh shall inherit all things; and I will be his God, and he shall be my son. 8. But the fearful, and unbelieving, and the abominable, and murderers, and whoremongers, and sorcerers, and idolaters, and all liars, shall have their part in the lake which burneth with fire and brimstone: which is the second death."*

This new heaven and new earth are free of tears, death, sorrow, crying, and pain. Our Lord has made that provision. He is faithful, and he gives freely. He is the author of all things that are good. We are sons of God. The eighth promise of Revelation is given to the overcomer. *"He that overcometh shall inherit all things; and I will be his God, and he shall be my son."* The last statement of warning reminds us of James' admonition. *"If any of lack wisdom, let him ask of God, that giveth to all men liberally, and upbraideth not; and it shall be given him. But let him ask in faith, nothing wavering. For he that wavereth is like a wave of the sea driven with the wind and tossed. For let not that man think that he shall receive any thing of the Lord. A double minded man is unstable in all his ways"* (James 1:5–8). The consequence of unbelief, pride, and sensual sin is eternal damnation.

VERSES 9–14: *9. "And there came unto me one of the seven angels which had the seven vials full of the seven last plagues, and talked with me, saying, Come hither, I will shew thee the bride, the Lamb's wife. 10. And he carried me away in the spirit to a great and high mountain, and shewed me that great city, the holy Jerusalem, descending out of heaven from God, 11. Having the glory of God: and her light was like unto a stone most precious, even like a jasper stone, clear as crystal; 12. And had a wall great and high, and had twelve gates, and at the gates twelve angels, and names written thereon, which are the names of the twelve tribes of the children of Israel: 13. On the east three gates; on the north three gates; on the south three gates; and on the west three gates. 14. And the wall of the city had twelve foundations, and in them the names of the twelve apostles of the Lamb."*

The angel invites John to see *"the bride, the Lamb's wife."* What John sees is *"that great city, the holy Jerusalem, descending out of heaven from God."* Paul identified the before-descending heavenly residence. *"But Jerusalem which is above is free, which is the mother of us all"* (Galatians 4:26). John sees the revealed fullness of God's *"intent."* That is his *"Word"* which was made flesh in Jesus Christ. Jesus is the *"Alpha and Omega"* of the whole matter. He has that by his Father's gift of *"all things."* It is his inheritance. The Father of faith, Abraham *"looked for a city which hath foundations, whose builder and maker is God"* (Hebrews 11:10).

VERSES 15–21: *15. "And he that talked with me had a golden reed to measure the city, and the gates thereof, and the wall thereof. 16. And the city lieth foursquare, and the length is as large as the breadth: and he measured the city with the reed, twelve thousand furlongs. The length and the breadth and the height of it are equal. 17. And he measured the wall thereof, an hundred and forty and four cubits, according to the measure of a man, that is, of the angel. 18. And the building of the wall of it was of jasper: and the city was pure gold, like unto clear glass. 19. And the foundations of the wall of the city were garnished with all manner of precious stones. The first foundation was jasper; the second, sapphire; the third, a chalcedony; the fourth, an emerald; 20. The fifth, sardonyx; the sixth, sardius; the seventh, chrysolite; the eighth, beryl; the ninth, a topaz; the tenth, a chrysoprasus; the eleventh, a jacinth; the twelfth, an amethyst. 21. And the twelve gates were twelve pearls; every several gate was of one pearl: and the street of the city was pure gold, as it were transparent glass."*

The event is over two thousand years future to John's time, but the vision is literal and it is real. Abraham and his seed will occupy the geography. That city and that geography will forever be God's. *"And the city had no need of the sun, neither of the moon, to shine in it: for the glory of God did lighten it, and the Lamb is the light thereof"* (verse 23).

VERSES 22–27: *22. "And I saw no temple therein: for the Lord God Almighty and the Lamb are the temple of it. 23. And the city had no need of the sun, neither of the moon, to shine in it: for the glory of God did lighten it, and the Lamb is the light thereof. 24. And the nations of them which are saved shall walk in the light of it: and the kings of the earth do bring their glory and honour into it. 25. And the gates of it shall not be shut at all by day: for there shall be no night there. 26. And they shall bring the glory and honour of the nations into it. 27. And there shall in no wise enter into it any thing that defileth, neither whatsoever worketh abomination, or maketh a lie: but they which are written in the Lamb's book of life."*

These verses declare that God and the Lamb are the abiding conscience of the new heaven and the new earth. It is purity and righteousness. The light of that city is perpetual and that is literal light as well as the light of the knowledge of God. The literal light will forever be the evidence and call to obedience and service to the righteous, mighty, and merciful God of heaven and the Lamb. *"For his mercy endureth for ever"* (Psalms).

CHAPTER 22: *1. "And he shewed me a pure river of water of life, clear as crystal, proceeding out of the throne of God and of the Lamb. 2. In the midst of the street of it, and on either side of the river, was there the tree of life, which bare twelve manner of fruits, and yielded her fruit every month: and the leaves of the tree were for the healing of the nations. 3. And there shall be no more curse: but the throne of God and of the Lamb shall be in it; and his servants shall serve him: 4. And they shall see his face; and his name shall be in their foreheads. 5. And there shall be no night there; and they need no candle, neither light of the sun; for the Lord God giveth them light: and they shall reign for ever and ever. 6. And he said unto me, These sayings are faithful and true: and the Lord God of the holy prophets sent his angel to shew unto his servants the things which must shortly be done. 7. Behold, I come quickly: blessed is he that keepeth the sayings of the prophecy of this book. 8. And I John saw these things, and heard them. And when I had heard and seen, I fell down to worship before the feet of the angel which shewed me these things. 9. Then saith he unto me, See thou do it not: for I am thy fellowservant, and of thy brethren the prophets, and of them which keep the sayings of this book: worship God. 10. And he saith unto me, Seal not the sayings of the prophecy of this book: for the time is at hand. 11. He that is unjust, let him be unjust still: and he which is filthy, let him be filthy still: and he that is righteous, let him be righteous still: and he that is holy, let him be holy still. 12. And, behold, I come quickly; and my reward is with me, to give every man according as his work shall be. 13. I am Alpha and Omega, the beginning and the end, the first and the last. 14. Blessed are they that do his commandments, that they may have right to the tree of life, and may enter in through the gates into the city. 15. For without are dogs, and sorcerers, and whoremongers, and murderers, and idolaters, and whosoever loveth and maketh a lie. 16. I Jesus have sent mine angel to testify unto you these things in the churches. I am the root and the offspring of David, and the bright and morning star. 17. And the Spirit and the bride say, Come. And let him that heareth say, Come. And let him that is athirst come. And whosoever will, let him take the water of life freely. 18. For I testify unto every man that heareth the words of the prophecy of this book, If any man shall add unto these things, God shall add unto him the plagues that are written in this book: 19. And if any man shall take away from the words of the book of this prophecy, God shall take away his part out of the book of life, and out of the holy city, and from the things which are written in this book. 20. He which testifieth these things saith, Surely I come quickly. Amen. Even so, come, Lord Jesus. 21. The grace of our Lord Jesus Christ be with you all. Amen."*

Chapter 22, as written, sufficiently reflects the message to the reader. Commentary is minimal.

In the light of a perfect day, John is admonished to receive and conform to the Lord God who is both author and finisher of all righteousness.

REVELATION, CHAPTERS 21-22

VERSES 1–5: *1. "And he shewed me a pure river of water of life, clear as crystal, proceeding out of the throne of God and of the Lamb. 2. In the midst of the street of it, and on either side of the river, was there the tree of life, which bare twelve manner of fruits, and yielded her fruit every month: and the leaves of the tree were for the healing of the nations. 3. And there shall be no more curse: but the throne of God and of the Lamb shall be in it; and his servants shall serve him: 4. And they shall see his face; and his name shall be in their foreheads. 5. And there shall be no night there; and they need no candle, neither light of the sun; for the Lord God giveth them light: and they shall reign for ever and ever."*

The vision of God's provision: Its origin is in heaven. God and the Lamb are the root and offspring. Righteousness and mercy have prevailed. The love of God is the light. The servants are loved of their master and the servants love the master. The servants have the mind of the Lord.

VERSES 6–10: *6. "And he said unto me, These sayings are faithful and true: and the Lord God of the holy prophets sent his angel to shew unto his servants the things which must shortly be done. 7. Behold, I come quickly: blessed is he that keepeth the sayings of the prophecy of this book. 8. And I John saw these things, and heard them. And when I had heard and seen, I fell down to worship before the feet of the angel which shewed me these things. 9. Then saith he unto me, See thou do it not: for I am thy fellowservant, and of thy brethren the prophets, and of them which keep the sayings of this book: worship God. 10. And he saith unto me, Seal not the sayings of the prophecy of this book: for the time is at hand."*

The angel addresses John at this time as unto a man admonished to embrace his commission. John's mandate is received, and he is worshipful. There is the flavor of expediency.

VERSES 11–17: *11. "He that is unjust, let him be unjust still: and he which is filthy, let him be filthy still: and he that is righteous, let him be righteous still: and he that is holy, let him be holy still. 12. And, behold, I come quickly; and my reward is with me, to give every man according as his work shall be. 13. I am Alpha and Omega, the beginning and the end, the first and the last. 14. Blessed are they that do his commandments, that they may have right to the tree of life, and may enter in through the gates into the city. 15. For without are dogs, and sorcerers, and whoremongers, and murderers, and idolaters, and whosoever loveth and maketh a lie. 16. I Jesus have sent mine angel to testify unto you these things in the churches. I am the root and the offspring of David, and the bright and morning star. 17. And the Spirit and the bride say, Come. And let him that heareth say, Come. And let him that is athirst come. And whosoever will, let him take the water of life freely."*

The time of atonement and salvation has come, and that door is closing. Jesus is the root and offspring. He is the *"Word"* and he is the *"Word"* made flesh. All that is outside of his auspices is fitted for destruction.

VERSES 18–21: *18. "For I testify unto every man that heareth the words of the prophecy of this book, If any man shall add unto these things, God shall add unto him the plagues that are written in this book: 19. And if any man shall take away from the words of the book of this prophecy, God shall take away his part out of the book of life, and out of the holy city, and from the things which are written in this book. 20. He which testifieth these things saith, Surely I come quickly. Amen. Even so, come, Lord Jesus. 21. The grace of our Lord Jesus Christ be with you all. Amen."*

CHAPTER XVIII
TABLES

The following tables begin with Revelation chapter 6 and end with chapter 18. The Scripture is given in parallel fashion so that the reader can compare the columns/Scripture with respect to timeline and from whom and to whom the declarations are addressed. And, from what realm, heaven or heaven-ordained Church administration.

TABLE I

Chapter 6 gives the heavenly viewpoint of the first four seals. Christ, on the white horse, is 'administrator.' The red horse reflects separation from Creator God, which is enmity, which is causal for warring. The black horse reflects loss of dominion of the plant kingdom resulting in famine. The pale horse reflects death and pestilence which resulted in the loss of dominion of the animal kingdom, both micro and macro. 'Enmity' is the mother of all curses. Chapter 8 shows the related transitioning into the earth of the seals; judgments spoken by angels and administered by the gifted Church. The first four seals occupy the first three and one-half years of the last hour. It is the time of the Latter Rain Gentile church.

The Revelation of Jesus Christ Pertaining to the Kingdom of God

CHAPTER 6. *1. "And I saw when the Lamb opened <u>one of the seals</u>, and I heard, as it were the noise of thunder, one of the four beasts saying, Come and see. 2. And I saw, and behold a white horse: and he that sat on him had a bow; and a crown was given unto him: and he went forth conquering, and to conquer.*

3. And when he had opened <u>the second seal</u>, I heard the second beast say, Come and see. 4. And there went out another horse that was red: and power was given to him that sat thereon to take peace from the earth, and that they should kill one another: and there was given unto him a great sword.

5. And when he had opened <u>the third seal</u>, I heard the third beast say, Come and see. And I beheld, and lo a black horse; and he that sat on him had a pair of balances in his hand. 6. And I heard a voice in the midst of the four beasts say, A measure of wheat for a penny, and three measures of barley for a penny; and see thou hurt not the oil and the wine. 7. And when he had opened <u>the fourth seal</u>, I heard the voice of the fourth beast say, Come and see. 8. And I looked, and behold a pale horse: and his name that sat on him was Death, and Hell followed with him. And power was given unto them over the fourth part of the earth, to kill with sword, and with hunger, and with death, and with the beasts of the earth."

CHAPTER 8. *2. "And I saw the seven angels which stood before God; and to them were given seven trumpets. 3. And another angel came and stood at the altar, having a golden censer; and there was given unto him much incense, that he should offer it with the prayers of all saints upon the golden altar which was before the throne. 4. And the smoke of the incense, which came with the prayers of the saints, ascended up before God out of the angel's hand. 5. And the angel took the censer, and filled it with fire of the altar, and cast it into the earth: and there were voices, and thunderings, and lightnings, and an earthquake. 6. And the seven angels which had the seven trumpets prepared themselves to sound. 7. <u>The first angel</u> sounded, and there followed hail and fire mingled with blood, and they were cast upon the earth: and the third part of trees was burnt up, and all green grass was burnt up. 8. And <u>the second angel</u> sounded, and as it were a great mountain burning with fire was cast into the sea: and the third part of the sea became blood; 9. And the third part of the creatures which were in the sea, and had life, died; and the third part of the ships were destroyed. 10. And <u>the third angel</u> sounded, and there fell a great star from heaven, burning as it were a lamp, and it fell upon the third part of the rivers, and upon the fountains of waters; 11. And the name of the star is called Wormwood: and the third part of the waters became wormwood; and many men died of the waters, because they were made bitter. 12. And <u>the fourth angel</u> sounded, and the third part of the sun was smitten, and the third part of the moon, and the third part of the stars; so as the third part of them was darkened, and the day shone not for a third part of it, and the night likewise. 13. And I beheld, and heard an angel flying through the midst of heaven, saying with a loud voice, Woe, woe, woe, to the inhabiters of the earth by reason of the other voices of the trumpet of the three angels, which are yet to sound!"*

TABLES

TABLE II

Chapter 6, beginning with verse 9, gives the fifth seal; heaven's accounting of the death of the saints and their blood crying out for justice. Chapter 9, beginning with verse 9, shows the related transitioning of the seal's judgment, spoken by angels, into the earth. The fifth and sixth seals occupy the second three and one-half years of the last hour.

| CHAPTER 6. 9. "And when he had opened <u>the fifth seal</u>, I saw under the altar the souls of them that were slain for the word of God, and for the testimony which they held: 10. And they cried with a loud voice, saying, How long, O Lord, holy and true, dost thou not judge and avenge our blood on them that dwell on the earth? 11. And white robes were given unto every one of them; and it was said unto them, that they should rest yet for a little season, until their fellow servants also and their brethren, that should be killed as they were, should be fulfilled.

12. And I beheld when he had opened <u>the sixth seal</u>, and, lo, there was a <u>great earthquake</u>; and the sun became black as sackcloth of hair, and the moon became as blood; 13. And the stars of heaven fell unto the earth, even as a fig tree casteth her untimely figs, when she is shaken of a mighty wind. 14. And the heaven departed as a scroll when it is rolled together; and every mountain and island were moved out of their places. 15. And the kings of the earth, and the great men, and the rich men, and the chief captains, and the mighty men, and every bondman, and every free man, hid themselves in the dens and in the rocks of the mountains; 16. And said to the mountains and rocks, Fall on us, and hide us from the face of him that sitteth on the throne, and from the wrath of the Lamb: 17. For the great day of his wrath is come; and who shall be able to stand?" | CHAPTER 9. *1. "And <u>the fifth angel</u> sounded, and I saw a star fall from heaven unto the earth: and to him was given the key of the bottomless pit. 2. And he opened the bottomless pit; and there arose a smoke out of the pit, as the smoke of a great furnace; and the sun and the air were darkened by reason of the smoke of the pit. 3. And there came out of the smoke locusts upon the earth: and unto*

them was given power, as the scorpions of the earth have power. 4. And it was commanded them that they should not hurt the grass of the

earth, neither any green thing, neither any tree; but only those men which have not the seal of God in their foreheads. 5. And to them it was given that they should not kill them, but that they should be tormented five months: and their torment was as the torment of a scorpion, when he striketh a man. 6. And in those days shall men seek death, and shall not find it; and shall desire to die, and death shall flee from them. 7. And the shapes of the locusts were like unto horses prepared unto battle; and on their heads were as it were crowns like gold, and their faces were as the faces of men. 8. And they had hair as the hair of women, and their teeth were as the teeth of lions. 9. And they had breastplates, as it were breastplates of iron; and the sound of their wings was as the sound of chariots of many horses running to battle. 10. And they had tails like unto scorpions, and there were stings in their tails: and ttheir power was to hurt men five months. 11. And they had a king over them, which is the angel of the bottomless pit, whose name in the Hebrew tongue is Abaddon, but in the Greek tongue hath his name Apollyon. 12. One woe is past; and, behold, there come two woes more hereafter. 13. And the sixth angel sounded, and I heard a voice from the four horns of the golden altar which is before God, 14. Saying to the sixth angel which had the trumpet, Euphrates. 15. And the four angels were loosed, which were prepared for an hour, and a day, and a month, and a year, for to slay the third part of men. 16. And the number of the army of the horsemen were two hundred thousand thousand: and I heard the number of them 17. And thus I saw the horses in the |

	vision, and them that sat on them, having breastplates of fire, and of jacinth, and brimstone: and the heads of the horses were as the heads of lions; and out of their mouths issued fire and smoke and brimstone. 18. By these three was the third part of men killed, by the fire, and by the smoke, and by the brimstone, which issued out of their mouths. 19. For their power is in their mouth, and in their tails: for their tails were like unto serpents, and had heads, and with them they do hurt. 20. And the rest of the men which were not killed by these plagues yet repented not of the works of their hands, that they should not worship devils, and idols of gold, and silver, and brass, and stone, and of wood: which neither can see, nor hear, nor walk: 21. Neither repented they of their murders, nor of their sorceries, nor of their fornication, nor of their thefts." CHAPTER 11, VERSES 11–14. *11. "And after three days and an half the Spirit of life from God entered into them, and they stood upon their feet; and great fear fell upon them which saw them. 12. And they heard a great voice from heaven saying unto them, Come up hither. And they ascended up to heaven in a cloud; and their enemies beheld them." 13. "And the same hour was there a <u>great earthquake</u>, and the tenth part of the city fell, and in the earthquake were slain of men seven thousand: and the remnant were affrighted, and gave glory to the God of heaven. 14. The second woe is past; and, behold, the third woe cometh quickly."*

Table III

Chapter 8, verse 1, states the opening of the seventh seal. Chapter 10 gives the mighty angel's declaration of the advent of the seventh seal. The seventh seal occupies seven and one-half years. It is the first seven and one-half years opening Christ's millennium reign.

TABLES

| CHAPTER 8. *1. "And when he had opened <u>the seventh seal</u>, there was silence in heaven about the space of half an hour."* | CHAPTER 10. *1. "And I saw another mighty angel (<u>the days of . . . the seventh angel</u>) come down from heaven, clothed with a cloud: and a rainbow was upon his head, and his face was as it were the sun, and his feet as pillars of fire: 2. And he had in his hand a little book open: and he set his right foot upon the sea, and his left foot on the earth, 3. And cried with a loud voice, as when a lion roareth: and when he had cried, seven thunders uttered their voices. 4. And when the seven thunders had uttered their voices, I was about to write: and I heard a voice from heaven saying unto me, Seal up those things which the seven thunders uttered, and write them not. 5. And the angel which I saw stand upon the sea and upon the earth lifted up his hand to heaven, 6. And sware by him that liveth for ever and ever, who created heaven, and the things that therein are, and the earth, and the things that therein are, and the sea, and the things which are therein, that there should be time no longer: 7. But in the days of the voice of <u>the seventh angel</u>, when he shall begin to sound, the mystery of God should be finished, as he hath declared to his servants the prophets."* |

TABLE IV

This table treats chapter 11 as a timeline. Here, we back up to the beginning of the first three-and-one-half-year period: the Latter Rain church operation. Commensurate with the church operation is the occupation of Jerusalem by Gentile powers for the sake of peacekeeping. Chapter 12 gives the accounting of the Church. This is the same time frame as the first three and one-half years of the last hour covered in Table I.

| CHAPTER 11. *1. "And there was given me a reed like unto a rod: and the angel stood, saying, Rise, and measure the temple of God, and the altar, and them that worship therein. 2. But the court which is without the temple leave out, and measure it not; for it is given unto the Gentiles: and the holy city shall they tread under foot forty and two months. 3. And I will give power unto my two witnesses, and they shall prophesy a thousand two hundred and threescore days, clothed in sackcloth. 4. These are the two olive trees, and the two candlesticks standing before the God of the earth. 5. And if any man will hurt them, fire proceedeth out of their mouth, and devoureth their enemies: and if any man will hurt them, he must in this manner be killed. 6. These have power to shut heaven, that it rain not in the days of their prophecy: and have power over waters to turn them to blood, and to smite the earth with all plagues, as often as they will."* | CHAPTER 12. *1. "And there appeared a great wonder in heaven; a woman clothed with the sun, and the moon under her feet, and upon her head a crown of twelve stars: 2. And she being with child cried, travailing in birth, and pained to be delivered."* |

TABLE V

This table addresses the 'finished' Latter Rain Gentile church operation and the resulting three and one-half years of martyrdom; both chapter 11 and chapter 12. This is the same time frame as the second three and one-half years of Table II.

CHAPTER 11. 7. *"And when they shall have finished their testimony, the beast that ascendeth out of the bottomless pit shall make war against them, and shall overcome them, and kill them. 8. And their dead bodies shall lie in the street of the great city, which spiritually is called Sodom and Egypt, where also our Lord was crucified. 9. And they of the people and kindreds and tongues and nations shall see their dead bodies three days and an half, and shall not suffer their dead bodies to be put in graves. 10. And they that dwell upon the earth shall rejoice over them, and make merry, and shall send gifts one to another; because these two prophets tormented them that dwelt on the earth."*	CHAPTER 12. 3. *"And there appeared another wonder in heaven; and behold a great red dragon, having seven heads and ten horns, and seven crowns upon his heads. 4. And his tail drew the third part of the stars of heaven, and did cast them to the earth: and the dragon stood before the woman which was ready to be delivered, for to devour her child as soon as it was born."*

TABLE VI

This table addresses the *"ascended,"* first resurrection, which marks the beginning of the reign of Christ. The *"great earthquake"* marks the end of the Gentile times. This second woe is two notes sounding the end of Gentile times and the beginning of the first seven and one-half years of the millennium reign of Christ. This second woe is not given a 'time frame.' It occurs in the last six months of the second three and one-half years of the first woe. See Table II.

CHAPTER 11. *11. "And after three days and an half the Spirit of life from God entered into them, and they stood upon their feet; and great fear fell upon them which saw them. 12. And they heard a great voice from heaven saying unto them, Come up hither. And they ascended up to heaven in a cloud; and their enemies beheld them. 13. And the same hour was there a great earthquake, and the tenth part of the city fell, and in the earthquake were slain of men seven thousand: and the remnant were affrighted, and gave glory to the God of heaven."*	CHAPTER 12. 5. *"And she brought forth a man child, who was to rule all nations with a rod of iron: and her child was caught up unto God, and to his throne. 6. And the woman fled into the wilderness, where she hath a place prepared of God, that they should feed her there a thousand two hundred and threescore days. 7. And there was war in heaven: Michael and his angels fought against the dragon; and the dragon fought and his angels, 8. And prevailed not; neither was their place found any more in heaven. 9. And the great dragon was cast out, that old serpent, called the Devil, and Satan, which deceiveth the whole world: he was cast out into the earth, and his angels were cast out with him."*

TABLES

TABLE VII

This table addresses the seventh angel/third and final woe. The time frame is the beginning seven and one-half years of the millennium reign of Christ. It is a period of seven and one-half years of seven thunders and seven vials poured out into the earth. The post-Rapture tribulation.

| CHAPTER 11. *14. "The second woe is past; and, behold, the third woe cometh quickly. 15. And the seventh angel sounded; <u>and there were great voices in heaven, saying</u>, The kingdoms of this world are become the kingdoms of our Lord, and of his Christ; and he shall reign for ever and ever. 16. And the four and twenty elders, which sat before God on their seats, fell upon their faces, and worshipped God, 17. Saying, We give thee thanks, O Lord God Almighty, which art, and wast, and art to come; because thou hast taken to thee thy great power, and hast reigned. 18. And the nations were angry, and thy wrath is come, and the time of the dead, that they should be judged, and that thou shouldest give reward unto thy servants the prophets, and to the saints, and them that fear thy name, small and great; and shouldest destroy them which destroy the earth. 19. And the temple of God was opened in heaven, and there was seen in his temple the ark of his testament: and there were lightnings, and voices, and thunderings, and an earthquake, and great hail."* | CHAPTER 12. *10. "And I heard <u>a loud voice saying in heaven</u>, Now is come salvation, and strength, and the kingdom of our God, and the power of his Christ: for the accuser of our brethren is cast down, which accused them before our God day and night. 11. And they overcame him by the blood of the Lamb, and by the word of their testimony; and they loved not their lives unto the death. 12. Therefore rejoice, ye heavens, and ye that dwell in them. Woe to the inhabiters of the earth and of the sea! for the devil is come down unto you, having great wrath, because he knoweth that he hath but a short time. 13. And when the dragon saw that he was cast unto the earth, he persecuted the woman which brought forth the man child. 14. And to the woman were given two wings of a great eagle, that she might fly into the wilderness, into her place, where she is nourished for a time, and times, and half a time, from the face of the serpent. 15. And the serpent cast out of his mouth water as a flood after the woman, that he might cause her to be carried away of the flood. 16. And the earth helped the woman, and the earth opened her mouth, and swallowed up the flood which the dragon cast out of his mouth. 17. And the dragon was wroth with the woman, and went to make war with the remnant of her seed, which keep the commandments of God, and have the testimony of Jesus Christ."* |

Table VII concludes our treatment of the timeline of the seals. The following tables VIII and IX, irrespective of a 'timeline,' treat the judgment of the seventh and eighth beasts. The following tables give Scripture showing the seventh seal/seventh angel occupying the first seven and one-half years of Christ's millennium reign.

TABLE VIII

This table shows Scripture pertaining to the seventh beast comprised of the ungodly sea of peoples of the Gentile world. And then, the eighth beast comprised of the same fallen humanity, but added to by the fallen spirits forces of the demonic realm.

The Revelation of Jesus Christ Pertaining to the Kingdom of God

CHAPTER 13. *1. "And I stood upon the sand of the sea, and saw a beast rise up out of the sea, having seven heads and ten horns, and upon his horns ten crowns, and upon his heads the name of blasphemy. 2. And the beast which I saw was like unto a leopard, and his feet were as the feet of a bear, and his mouth as the mouth of a lion: and the dragon gave him his power, and his seat, and great authority. 3. And I saw one of his heads as it were wounded to death; and his deadly wound was healed: and all the world wondered after the beast. 4. And they worshipped the dragon which gave power unto the beast: and they worshipped the beast, saying, Who is like unto the beast? who is able to make war with him? 5. And there was given unto him a mouth speaking great things and blasphemies; and power was given unto him to continue forty and two months. 6. And he opened his mouth in blasphemy against God, to blaspheme his name, and his tabernacle, and them that dwell in heaven. 7. And it was given unto him to make war with the saints, and to overcome them: and power was given him over all kindreds, and tongues, and nations. 8. And all that dwell upon the earth shall worship him, whose names are not written in the book of life of the Lamb slain from the foundation of the world. 9. If any man have an ear, let him hear. 10. He that leadeth into captivity shall go into captivity: he that killeth with the sword must be killed with the sword. Here is the patience and the faith of the saints. 11. And I beheld another beast <u>coming up out of the earth</u>; and he had two horns like a lamb, and he spake as a dragon. 12. And he exerciseth all the power of the first beast before him, and causeth the earth and them which dwell therein to worship the first beast, whose deadly wound was healed. 13. And he doeth great wonders, so that he maketh fire come down from heaven on the earth in the sight of men, 14. And deceiveth them that dwell on the earth by the means of those miracles which he had power to do in the sight of the beast; saying to them that dwell on the earth, that they should make an image to the beast, which had the wound by a sword, and did live. 15. And he had power to give life unto the image of the beast, that the image of the beast should both speak, and cause that as many as would not worship the image of the beast should be killed. 16. And he causeth all, both small and great, rich and poor, free and bond, to receive a mark in their right hand, or in their foreheads: 17. And that no man might buy or sell, save he that had the mark, or the name of the beast, or the number of his name. 18. Here is wisdom. Let him that hath understanding count the number of the beast: for it is the*

CHAPTER 17. *1. "And there came one of the seven angels which had the seven vials, and talked with me, saying unto me, Come hither; I will shew unto thee the judgment of the great whore that sitteth upon many waters: 2. With whom the kings of the earth have committed fornication, and the inhabitants of the earth have been made drunk with the wine of her fornication. 3. So he carried me away in the spirit into the wilderness: and I saw a woman sit upon a scarlet coloured beast, full of names of blasphemy, having seven heads and ten horns. 4. And the woman was arrayed in purple and scarlet colour, and decked with gold and precious stones and pearls, having a golden cup in her hand full of abominations and filthiness of her fornication: 5. And upon her forehead was a name written, MYSTERY, BABYLON THE GREAT, THE MOTHER OF HARLOTS AND ABOMINATIONS OF THE EARTH. 6. And I saw the woman drunken with the blood of the saints, and with the blood of the martyrs of Jesus: and when I saw her, I wondered with great admiration. 7. And the angel said unto me, Wherefore didst thou marvel? I will tell thee the mystery of the woman, and of the beast that carrieth her, which hath the seven heads and ten horns. 8. The beast that thou sawest was, and is not; and shall <u>ascend out of the bottomless pit</u>, and go into perdition: and they that dwell on the earth shall wonder, whose names were not written in the book of life from the foundation of the world, when they behold the beast that was, and is not, and yet is. 9. And here is the mind which hath wisdom. The seven heads are seven mountains, on which the woman sitteth. 10. And there are seven kings: five are fallen, and one is, and the other is not yet come; and when he cometh, he must continue a short space. 11. And the beast that was, and is not, even he is the eighth, and is of the seven, and goeth into perdition. 12. And the ten horns which thou sawest are ten kings, which have received no kingdom as yet; but receive power as kings one hour with the beast. 13. These have one mind, and shall give their power and strength unto the beast. 14. These shall make war with the Lamb, and the Lamb shall overcome them: for he is Lord of lords, and King of kings: and they that are with him are called, and chosen, and faithful. 15. And he saith unto me, The waters which thou sawest, where the whore sitteth, are peoples, and multitudes, and nations, and tongues. 16. And the ten horns which thou sawest upon the beast, these shall hate the whore, and shall make her desolate and naked, and shall eat.*

TABLES

number of a man; and his number is Six hundred three-score and six."	*her flesh, and burn her with fire. 17. For God hath put in their hearts to fulfil his will, and to agree, and give their kingdom unto the beast, until the words of God shall be fulfilled. 18. And the woman which thou sawest is that great city, which reigneth over the kings of the earth."*

TABLE IX

This table gives Scripture addressing the time of the third woe and introduction of the seventh seal/seventh angel. It is the first seven and one-half years of Christ's millennium reign. The third woe includes seven thunders and seven vials poured into the earth. It is the cleansing wrath of God.

Table IX concludes the chapter of tables. Beyond the third woe, ending with Armageddon, is the continuing "seventh." It is the everlasting kingdom of Christ, the seventh angel.

CHAPTER 8. *1. "And when he had opened the seventh seal, there was silence in heaven about the space of half an hour."* CHAPTER 11. *14. "The second woe is past; and, behold, the third woe cometh quickly.* *15. And the seventh angel sounded; and there were great voices in heaven, saying, The kingdoms of this world are become the kingdoms of our Lord, and of his Christ; and he shall reign for ever and ever. 16. And the four and twenty elders, which sat before God on their seats, fell upon their faces, and worshipped God, 17. Saying, We give thee thanks, O Lord God Almighty, which art, and wast, and art to come; because thou hast taken to thee thy great power, and hast reigned. 18. And the nations were angry, and thy wrath is come, and the time of the dead, that they should be judged, and that thou shouldest give reward unto thy servants the prophets, and to the saints, and them that fear thy name, small and great; and shouldest destroy them which destroy the earth. 19. And the temple of God was opened in heaven, and there was seen in his temple the ark of his testament: and there were lightnings, and voices, and thunderings, and an earthquake, and great hail."* CHAPTER 15. *1. "And I saw another sign in heaven, great and marvelous, seven angels having the seven last plagues; for in them is filled up the wrath of God. 2. And I saw as it were a sea of glass mingled with fire: and them that had gotten the victory over the beast,*	

and over his image, and over his mark, and over the number of his name, stand on the sea of glass, having the harps of God. 3. And they sing the song of Moses the servant of God, and the song of the Lamb, saying, Great and marvelous are thy works, Lord God Almighty; just and true are thy ways, thou King of saints. 4. Who shall not fear thee, O Lord, and glorify thy name? for thou only art holy: for all nations shall come and worship before thee; for thy judgments are made manifest. 5. And after that I looked, and, behold, the temple of the tabernacle of the testimony in heaven was opened: 6. And the seven angels came out of the temple, having the seven plagues, clothed in pure and white linen, and having their breasts girded with golden girdles. 7. And one of the four beasts gave unto the seven angels seven golden vials full of the wrath of God, who liveth for ever and ever. 8. And the temple was filled with smoke from the glory of God, and from his power; and no man was able to enter into the temple, till the seven plagues of the seven angels were fulfilled."

CHAPTER 16. *1. "And I heard a <u>great voice</u> out of the temple saying to the seven angels, Go your ways, and pour out the vials of the wrath of God upon the earth. 2. And the first went, and poured out his vial upon the earth; and there fell a noisome and grievous sore upon the men which had the mark of the beast, and upon them which worshipped his image. 3. And the second angel poured out his vial upon the sea; and it became as the blood of a dead man: and every living soul died in the sea. 4. And the third angel poured out his vial upon the rivers and fountains of waters; and they became blood. 5. And I heard the angel of the waters say, Thou art righteous, O Lord, which art, and wast, and shalt be, because thou hast judged thus. 6. For they have shed the blood of saints and prophets, and thou hast given them blood to drink; for they are worthy. 7. And I heard another out of the altar say, Even so, Lord God Almighty, true and righteous are thy judgments. 8. And the fourth angel poured out his vial upon the sun; and power was given unto him to scorch men with fire. 9. And men were scorched with great heat, and blasphemed the name of God, which hath power over these plagues: and they repented not to give him glory. 10. And the fifth angel poured out his vial upon the seat of the beast; and his kingdom was full of darkness; and they gnawed*

CHAPTER 14. *1. "And I looked, and, lo, a Lamb stood on the mount Sion, and with him an hundred forty and four thousand, having his Father's name written in their foreheads. 2. And I heard a voice from heaven, as the voice of many waters, and as the voice of a great thunder: and I heard the voice of harpers harping with their harps: 3. And they sung as it were a new song before the throne, and before the four beasts, and the elders: and no man could learn that song but the hundred and forty and four thousand, which were redeemed from the earth. 4. These are they which were not defiled with women; for they are virgins. These are they which follow the Lamb whithersoever he goeth. These were redeemed from among men, being the firstfruits unto God and to the Lamb. 5. And in their mouth was found no guile: for they are without fault before the throne of God.*

6. And I saw another angel fly in the midst of heaven, having the everlasting gospel to preach unto them that dwell on the earth, and to every nation, and kindred, and tongue, and people, 7. Saying with a loud voice, Fear God, and give glory to him; for the hour of his judgment is come: and worship him that made heaven, and earth, and the sea, and the fountains of waters. 8. And there followed another angel, saying, Babylon is fallen, is fallen, that great city, because she made all nations drink of the wine of the wrath of her fornication. 9. And the third angel followed them, saying with a loud voice, If any man worship the beast and his image, and receive his mark in his forehead, or in his hand, 10. The same shall drink of the wine of the wrath of God, which is poured out without mixture into the cup of his indignation; and he shall be tormented with fire and brimstone in the presence of the holy angels, and in the presence of the Lamb: 11. And the smoke of their torment ascendeth up for ever and ever: and they have no rest day nor night, who worship the beast and his image, and whosoever receiveth the mark of his name. 12. Here is the patience of the saints: here are they that keep the commandments of God, and the faith of Jesus. 13. And I heard a voice from heaven saying unto me, Write, Blessed are the dead which die in the Lord from henceforth:

Yea, saith the Spirit, that they may rest from their labors; and their works do follow them. 14. And I looked, and behold a white cloud, and upon the their tongues for pain, 11. And blasphemed the God of heaven because of their pains and their sores, and repented not of their deeds. 12. And the sixth angel poured out his vial upon the great river Euphrates; and the water thereof was dried up, that the way of the kings of the east might be prepared. 13. And I saw three unclean spirits like frogs come out of the mouth of the dragon, and out of the mouth of the beast, and out of the mouth of the false prophet. 14. For they are the spirits of devils, working miracles, which go forth unto the kings of the earth and of the whole world, to gather them to the battle of that great day of God Almighty. 15. Behold, I come as a thief. Blessed is he that watcheth, and keepeth his garments, lest he walk naked, and they see his shame. 16. And he gathered them together into a place called in the Hebrew tongue Armageddon. 17. And the seventh angel poured out his vial into the air; and there came a great voice out of the temple of heaven, from the throne, saying, It is done. 18. And there were voices, and thunders, and lightnings; and there was a great earthquake, such as was not since men were upon the earth, so mighty an earthquake, and so great. 19. And the great city was divided into three parts, and the cities of the nations fell: and great Babylon came in remembrance before God, to give unto her the cup of the wine of the fierceness of his wrath. 20. And every island fled away, and the mountains were not found. 21. And there fell upon men a great hail out of heaven, every stone about the weight of a talent: and men blasphemed God because of the plague of the hail; for the plague thereof was exceeding great."

cloud one sat like unto the Son of man, having on his head a golden crown, and in his hand a sharp sickle. 15. And another angel came out of the temple, crying with a loud voice to him that sat on the cloud, Thrust in thy sickle, and reap: for the time is come for thee to reap; for the harvest of the earth is ripe. 16. And he that sat on the cloud thrust in his sickle on the earth; and the earth was reaped. 17. And another angel came out of the temple which is in heaven, he also having a sharp sickle. 18. And another angel came out from the altar, which had power over fire; and cried with a loud cry to him that had the sharp sickle, saying, Thrust in thy sharp sickle, and gather the clusters of the vine of the earth; for her grapes are fully ripe. 19. And the angel thrust in his sickle into the earth, and gathered the vine of the earth, and cast it into the great winepress of the wrath of God. 20. And the winepress was trodden without the city, and blood came out of the winepress, even unto the horse bridles, by the space of a thousand and six hundred furlongs."

CHAPTER 18. *1. "And after these things I saw another angel come down from heaven, having great power; and the earth was lightened with his glory. 2. And he cried mightily with a <u>strong voice</u>, saying, Babylon the great is fallen, is fallen, and is become the habitation of devils, and the hold of every foul spirit, and a cage of every unclean and hateful bird. 3. For all nations have drunk of the wine of the wrath of her fornication, and the kings of the earth have committed fornication with her, and the merchants of the earth are waxed rich through the abundance of her delicacies. 4. And I heard another voice from heaven, saying, Come out of her, my people, that ye be not partakers of her sins, and that ye receive not of her plagues. 5. For her sins have reached unto heaven, and God hath remembered her iniquities. 6. Reward her even as she rewarded you, and double unto her double according to her works: in the cup which she hath filled fill to her double. 7. How much she hath glorified herself, and lived deliciously, so much torment and sorrow give her: for she saith in her heart, I sit a queen, and am no widow, and shall see no sorrow. 8. Therefore shall her plagues come in one day, death, and mourning, and famine; and she shall be utterly burned with fire: for strong is the Lord God who judgeth her. 9. And the kings of the earth, who have committed fornication and lived deliciously with her, shall bewail her, and lament for her, when they shall see the smoke of her burning, 10. Standing afar off for the fear of her torment, saying, Alas, alas,* *that great city Babylon, that mighty city! for in one hour is thy judgment come. 11. And the merchants of the earth shall weep and mourn over her; for no man buyeth their merchandise any more: 12. The merchandise of gold, and silver, and precious stones, and of pearls, and fine linen, and purple, and silk, and scarlet, and all thyine wood, and all manner vessels of ivory, and all manner vessels of most precious wood, and of brass, and iron, and marble, 13. And cinnamon, and odours, and ointments, and frankincense, and wine, and oil, and fine flour, and wheat, and beasts, and sheep, and horses, and chariots, and slaves, and souls of men. 14. And the fruits that thy soul lusted after are departed from thee, and all things which were dainty and goodly are departed from thee, and thou shalt find them no more at all. 15. The merchants of these things, which were made rich by her, shall stand afar off for the fear of her torment, weeping and wailing, 16. And saying, Alas, alas, that great city, that was clothed in fine linen, and purple, and scarlet, and decked with gold, and precious stones, and pearls! 17. For in one hour so great riches is come to nought. And every shipmaster, and all the company in ships, and sailors, and as many as trade by sea, stood afar off, 18. And cried when they saw the smoke of her burning, saying, What city is like unto this great city! 19. And they cast dust on their heads, and cried, weeping and wailing, saying, Alas, alas, that great city, wherein were made rich all that had ships in the sea by reason of her costliness! for in one hour is she made desolate. 20. Rejoice over her, thou heaven, and ye holy apostles and prophets; for God hath avenged you on her. 21. And a mighty angel took up a stone like a great millstone, and cast it into the sea, saying, Thus with violence shall that great city Babylon be thrown down, and shall be found no more at all. 22. And the voice of harpers, and musicians, and of pipers, and trumpeters, shall be heard no more at all in thee; and no craftsman, of whatsoever craft he be, shall be found any more in thee; and the sound of a millstone shall be heard no more at all in thee; 23. And the light of a candle shall shine no more at all in thee; and the voice of the bridegroom and of the bride shall be heard no more at all in thee: for thy merchants were the great men of the earth; for by thy sorceries were all nations deceived. 24. And in her was found the blood of prophets, and of saints, and of all that were slain upon the earth."*

Postscript

Prophecy occupies about one-third of the Bible. The fulfillment of prophecy is one proof positive that Scripture is divine in origin and inerrant. Commentary, however complete, falls short of the divine. This writer's treatment of Revelation is not exhaustive, nor was it meant to be. However, it is expressed with godly fear and awe and the expressions are truthful and sincere. Assessments and suggestions are not meant to be offensive or misleading, nor set forth with malice or hurt. Christian apologetics, at its best, must be flavored with a similarly confessed awareness, *"So likewise ye, when ye shall have done all those things which are commanded you, say, We are unprofitable servants: we have done that which was our duty to do"* (Luke 17:10). Knowing this benefit: Rightly understanding Scripture lends itself to an effectual embrace of God's Word, his plan, and his intent.